Freedom to Say YES

What it Takes to Stand by Your Values, Strengthen Your Identity, and Live Life Driven

BY

JIM RILEY

Ordering Information: Quantity sales. Special discounts are available on quantity purchases by corporations, associations, and others. Orders by U.S. trade bookstores and wholesalers.

www.DreamStartersPublishing.com

Table Of Contents

Advanced Praise

For Jim Riley and The Freedom to Say Yes

There is something about Jim that hits you right away. A depth, a passion, a true drive to be a man of purpose in this world. I felt it right away! I first met Jim when I was a Guest on his podcast “The Answer is Yes”. I was on a PR tour for my book “Fail Proof” after a successful run-on American Ninja Warrior and traveling around as a Keynote Speaker.

The podcast interview was great - but as I mentioned - there was something different that hit me right away. It’s Jim’s character. His presence. His commitment to be a man of faith, family, and country - all while truly supporting others to reach their goals.

I found that Jim and I are aligned in many areas of our lives and have a similar drive to succeed. We created a fast friendship and a bond amongst athletes and professionals in a non-conventual time in the country.

Jim lives a big, bold life centered upon his unshakable values. He is a man I deeply admire and feel very grateful to call my friend.

I look forward to catching up on Jim’s stories in this book, as well as continuing to develop our fast friendship. We are better together on this journey through life. It is easy to say “Yes” when people are willing to share in your passion - and Jim is that person.

Alex Weber
Award-Winning Speaker, TV Host, Author, and American Ninja Warrior.

Jim and I spent many hours together during the ‘good old days’ of corporate outings for a couple of companies we were both involved with. I always enjoyed my time with Jim who was smart, creative and someone who could ‘figure it out’. I know you’ll enjoy reading about Jim’s journey through his many business ventures.

Peter Jacobsen
Senior PGA Tour Golfer and Sports Announcer

I met Jim as a guest on his Just Say Yes podcast. We seemed to have an instant connection. Over the years I’ve come to discover that most everyone feels that way once they meet and work with Jim.

Let’s ponder his theme, The Freedom to say Yes! I’m convinced, today more than ever, this is a mantra humanity needs.

Why? For so many, this is the crucial choice: To settle for less, or to take action and get on track for success. And why so often do we choose to stay stuck?

Simple answer: We choose to stay right where we're at because it's easier than facing our fears. We choose to stay unhappy and dissatisfied and on the path of least resistance because it's easier than taking a risk.

Case in point: Do you have a vision for your life? Do you have dreams, goals and aspirations and yet, find yourself frequently falling short when it comes to turning those dreams into reality?

You will find the answers you are looking for with Jim. He has an uncanny ability to listen and then pinpoint exactly where the missing link is. He literally helps you connect the dots so you can create success in all areas of your life.

Working with Jim, you will find the Freedom to say Yes! and your life will be transformed!

Leslie Zann

Author of Outrageous Achievement and Speaker

For a variety of sometimes very complicated reasons, many of us have missed out on opportunities and life experiences because of our inability or fear to say "yes."

In Freedom to Say YES, Jim opens up about his life and the values he distilled in a life of saying yes when others were saying no, or nothing at all. Whenever I read a book I hope for at least one good take away, one thing I can fall back on and apply to my own life in a practical way. Jim gives his readers one in every chapter with illustrations that make his experiences your own.

More than a self-help, or business book, Freedom to Say YES, takes us back to the much needed, often overlooked virtue of having an identifiable value system; a system that exudes confidence, creates energy, and propels momentum. If you are ready to supercharge your life, or if you just need a tune up, Jim Riley's book is a must in your library. Better yet, buy several copies and pass them out to people you care about.

Rod Kuntz

Entrepreneur and Author of W.A.R.P.A.T.H. Alliance

Foreword

"If you're lost, go do something good for someone else, what you will find is purpose and passion."

That was a quote that I shared in a recent newsletter, and one that resonates with me deeply. I have been fortunate to have had several different careers in my life, but one thing that has always come through is my mission to empower others to be happy. More than that, I am on a mission to empower over 1 billion people to be happy, sharing strategies and tools for success, so we can scale happiness across the planet. Whether that is through coaching, my podcast, or speaking to an audience of thousands of people, I receive the most joy getting to know the impact that my clients and business colleagues have on the world.

Thanks to a career that has spanned the legal, technology, and sports industries, I've been able to connect with some of the world's top performers, from billionaires to Hall of Fame athletes, and beyond. What those interactions over the years have helped me to understand is that these people all have one thing in common: they have a desire that they must become who they can become. They are driven to fulfill their potential, and that is something that I saw in Jim Riley when I first met him.

I connected with Jim on my top business podcast, “The Playbook”, where I got to learn about how his mindset played into his successful racing career for Ford Motor Company in the Baja 1000 Off Road Race series. It was clear that we were aligned, and this brief encounter opened the door for me to work with Jim as a business client. Throughout his time as a client, I taught him some of my key principles such as “Ask and Attract”, “Say Thank You Every Morning and Night”, “Value for Value (aka the 100/20 Rule)” and many more. Jim also applied his key philosophy of having the “Freedom to say Yes” when it came to launching his podcast into a consulting business, after I had suggested it. I’ve always been impressed with Jim’s ability to be organized for our meetings and have a plan of attack to get things done. He’s always voted for “Faith over Fear” and understands the importance of time and execution in business.

Now, I have the pleasure of calling Jim a friend and he’s become someone that I can call on when needed. He often has our clients to be guests on his podcast show “The Answer is Yes” and is quick to tell them about his experience while working with me and the lessons he’s learned. It’s great to see that Jim understands the right approach to any situation, he’s a person who takes the perspective that he “gets to do things” instead of that he’s “got to do things”. It’s been an honor to be a part of Jim's journey writing this book and I would expect that there will be much more to come. Here's to leading like and champion and choosing to set the example for others to follow.

David Meltzer

Introduction

At the age of 12 I had very few friends in school, I lived in a 500sq ft apartment with my mom, and we were getting meals supplemented by the church. My Mom had incredible friends that helped support us and made us feel comfortable around the holidays. I remember the rent was $115 dollars a month and if we had enough gas to go to the river over the weekend, times were good. I never dreamed of a life more than what we had. And then I grew up…

My business partner, Bill Walton, would often tell me that I was driven all the time. While others would literally fall by the wayside in business and sports. I manage to find energy in areas that most people cannot pull from. In my mind, I never wanted an opportunity to pass me by.

"Being driven has been my second nature for longer than I can remember."

Life is too short to sit back and relax while my past does not define me. I have managed to find business opportunities or ways to stay entertained since the age of 13. I have sold gum on the school playground or washed cars with my mobile detail business. In my mind, I never wanted to rely on someone else to feed or cloth me if I could work. I also knew that if I wanted something, I would have to earn the money to buy it.

My dad taught me the value of putting in a hard day's work and earning money no matter what the job was. I perfected that at the age of 14 while working for my grandfather in his restaurant along the Newport Beach Harbor. I literally worked hard and played harder in my youth.

When I was sixteen and old enough to get a real job, on the books of life, I was already years ahead of my peers. I was a natural on the job and had an attitude to prove it. I made great money and learned how to climb the company ladder. My Brother Mark even encouraged me to play golf with some of the executives to "get ahead". That's about the time I was told that sometimes it's more important to listen, than speak my mind. I wish that advice had stuck, it did not! I was making six figures by the time I was twenty-five and spending that money like I was on a vacation seven days a week. My mouth and my money had created bigger problems than I could handle by the time I was 28 years old. I needed a change!

Fast Forward - No one knows when our time will come to depart, and that means that there is literally no better moment to do something than now. That's one way to look at things. I decided to first figure out what it was that kept me in that forever-driven state. The reason for that is quite simple; I wanted to unearth that reason, learn it, understand it, and then teach it to the rest of the world.

We live in harsher times where everything is changing at a rapid pace. From communication to business, we are constantly being bombarded with change. Keeping pace isn't exactly a choice anymore, but it is a necessity for anyone who wishes to keep on achieving success. The trouble is that while everyone wishes to do what is necessary, people tend to lose their drive, their passion, and end up accepting the idea that they cannot go any further. This is why you would see many settling down with the idea of retirement as long as they make the 401k by the end of the road. That isn't enough, especially not if you are aiming to do something big, something more significant in life, and lead a life with a purpose.

What is your purpose? Our purpose is not only to grow up, go through college, acquire a degree, work, pay taxes, retire, and die. Our purpose is larger, far more significant, and far more rewarding than any of these. As entrepreneurs, business owners, and professionals, we have what it takes to make a difference, but it is somewhere in the middle that most of us tend to give up the chase because we no longer have clarity in life. Our purpose, whatever it may be, starts evading us, and since we are not growing any younger, we find ourselves no longer driven towards our goals. We just settle for what we have, justify that it wasn't "meant for us," and move on. **For me, that was never the option, and it should not be for you either**.

I have always had goals, and have always gone after them, almost to a fault. Back when I was young, objects were significantly more important to me than family, kids, and values. I was that kid who dreamed about owning a car when he turned 16. As it turns out, I bought myself a new Ford Ranger off the lot, brand new. I risked it all, I co-signed for my parents without them knowing, wrote a check for a down payment, and my credit cleared. Nobody was going to keep me from the vison I had of driving into the school parking lot in a new truck and getting in trouble by my parents. My dreams became my reality.

Now, people often believe that if they think about something hard enough, visualize it every day, that they will go on to achieve their goals and desires. Not quite, there is a vital element that is missing. You must visualize and **then you become driven to put in the work**. Only after that do you end up achieving the results. So, if this was a formula, it would look something like this:

Visualization + Action = Results

I would do that for everything in life, whether it was a toy, a vehicle, a job, or even a job title. My entire life was always about me being driven towards my goals and achieving them. That's who I am.

Some of you may know me through my podcast series "*The Answer is Yes*" and that's where I have spoken at length about how you should say yes to opportunities in life. You never know what that opportunity can turn into. For example, you may be applying for a job that may not be right for you, given your lack of expertise or experience in that area. You end up getting a job offer. Most would actually turn it down out of fear and intimidation.

"What if I don't perform well?"
"I don't think I deserve this."
"I may not be the right person for this job."

STOP! Instead, say yes to it first and learn the skills later. It's fairly easy to acquire the skills later, and you can trust me on that one. Most companies have incredible training programs in place. The opportunity and being at the right place at the right time is the hard part to find. There is no point in spending days and weeks learning a skill only to find out that you cannot get yourself a job offer. If you find one before, take it, learn from it, and then grow.

I have lived a life of saying yes, and what's more interesting is that the more entrepreneurs I interview on my podcast, the more I realize just how they live with the same principles. They are the kind of people who go on to take the opportunity as it comes, with no second thoughts at all. They say yes to all opportunities simply to discover if these opportunities would go on to prove beneficial for them in one way or another. Even if these opportunities were a dead-end, there would be no regret. You don't know until you say yes to an opportunity and you chase that!

Throughout this book, I will coach, teach, and encourage readers just what it takes to become driven, to have that "I'll take it" attitude, and to live with a purpose. Through my personal experiences, stories, and the life lessons that I picked up along the way, I will provide a deep insight into what makes me say "yes" and why am I always driven towards my goals. This book will go on to become a conversation starter, an icebreaker, a tool, for those who wish to change the way they are living, who believe they have lost a purpose in life, or have yet to find one. If you are struggling to say yes to opportunities that present themselves to you, I assure you it is a lot easier than you might think.

I will share my values, and I will help you discover your own values, apply the lessons that you learn, and rediscover life with a completely new purpose, one that leads you towards a fulfilled destiny. If I can get just one person to experience a change in their lives, that's reward enough for me!

There are many entrepreneurs who have approached me for coaching, especially the ones who have come up with an idea but aren't exactly sure how to get that idea off the ground. Throughout my career, I have helped many people through the transition period, helping them to grow from a small business to a bigger one. These are the people who are willing to finally step out of the darkness, willing to change their lives, and those around them, and are happy to put in the work. All they need is a bit of guidance, directions, and some help to jump-start their careers. Of course, this isn't only restricted to business transitions. It is possible that some may wish to become a better version of themselves, looking towards a positive personal development and growth goal. That is where I come in, as a life coach, and as a mentor.

To give you an idea of what I am talking about, I want to paint you a picture of one of my clients. I was recently working with a professional softball player who was ready to compete on the biggest stage of them all – the Olympics. Only recently did she learn that softball was completely taken off the 2024 Olympics, and that left her devastated. By 2028, when they will eventually play softball again, she will no longer be eligible. This obviously threw a wrench into her life. Now, she needed a transition. Working with her, I am helping her to move smoothly into the world of business. With a little adjustment, and a dash of the right information, she will be able to harness *what makes her great* in softball and apply it to the business world in perpetuity. If she says YES to the opportunities that come her way of course.

Before you turn the page, ask yourself if you are ready. Ask yourself if you are someone who can truly use some guidance, some assistance, to make that important transition in life. Ask yourself if you will capitalize on an opportunity when it presents itself. Whether business or personal, if you really need to bring that change and achieve a sense of fulfillment in life, saddle up now. This is your opportunity, right here. Are you ready? Having ***The Freedom to Say Yes*** is how it all begins.

Romans 12: 9-12 (ESV)

9 Let love be genuine. Abhor what is evil; hold fast to what is
good. 10 Love one another with brotherly affection. Outdo one
another in showing honor. 11 Do not be slothful in zeal, be fervent
in spirit, serve the Lord. 12 Rejoice in hope, be patient in
tribulation, be constant in prayer.

Chapter 1

What You Believe is What You Will Achieve

"What you believe, is what you will achieve."

Mark Victor Hansen

The first real job I had was *with **In-N-Out Burger***. With that said, it certainly wasn't my first-ever job. I have been working ever since I turned 8 years old. Whether it was hustling gum sales on the school playground or selling rock band buttons, I was always looking to make that extra bit of money. In hindsight, I was an entrepreneur in the making.

Even though I always had the drive to push myself, I didn't really notice it until *In-N-Out Burger*. Incredibly, I went on to become one of the most successful store managers as I was the first person to sell over 1 million hamburgers in a single location in ONE year. One of the greatest things about that operation is how much they value their employees. They consider their employees as their most important assets, and I am not saying this to win any favors with them either.

Throughout my career there, I noticed how much they actually cared about us. This would be something that I would adopt in every one of my businesses going forward.

While I later went on to leave that job, I took with me many core values and practices. Just like I was treated as a genuine asset to the firm, I continue the same practice with my employees, with my business, the companies I helped, started, and ran. In-N-Out Burger even brought motivational speakers to talk to us. This was when I started to connect the dots between business (at any level) and personal development.

We had speakers like Pat Riley, Tommy Lasorda, all of whom were legendary icons in their respective fields of sports. We also met Mark Victor Hansen, a massive motivational speaker. He had a series called "How to Achieve Total Prosperity." For anyone who may not know who this person is, he is the co-author of the critically acclaimed book *Chicken Soup for the Soul*. This was around 1983.

There was something that Mark said that immediately resonated with me. He said:

"What you believe is what you will achieve."

I didn't waste a single second to take note of that. In the days that followed, I focused more on what he said and realized just how powerful and meaningful that a single sentence was. For the rest of my life, even today, I have lived in line with that sentence. I believe that whatever I can put my mind to, I can achieve it. It could be anything from acquiring new vehicles, jobs, houses, apartments, or even making big money. As long as I put my mind to it, I WILL achieve it, period.

Pushing Through

Your age can be the perfect motivation to get things done. When I turned 40, I thought to myself how incredible it would be for me to go on and achieve 40 different goals for my 40th birthday. That's a huge number of goals, but I believed I could do it and went for it. The trick is to figure out how to make the chase fun.

Obviously, my life has always been about chasing my goals and seeing them to fruition. Throughout my life, I have set myself goals that many would deam as impossible, and I went on to achieve every single one of them. The idea of achieving 40 goals was both refreshing and motivational for me. Of course, it was going to be challenging, but I was up for it, nonetheless.

One of the goals that I had set for myself was to climb *Mt. Rainier*. While it may seem like I was pushing my luck a bit too much here, or at least that's how most would think, I had a good climbing experience because I had been climbing Half Dome in Yosemite with my brother Mark Taylor.

He had a yearly outing with his management team. The idea was to camp in the village at Yosemite. Around 1 AM in the morning, we would leave our tents and we would run to the top of the Half Dome, and be there for the sunrise. Once that was done, we would run back down to the village.

The best part would be to run into people who had just started their ascend. They would often ask where we were coming from. When told that we were on our way back from the top, they would simply not believe us at all because we had already been there and were coming back right about the time where most traditional hikers would start their adventure. It was wild to see the shock in their eyes.

With my climbing experience, I decided Mt. Rainier would be the ideal achievement to accomplish. If you have ever flown across Seattle, Washington, it is a massive, daunting mountain, with a glacier, that overlooks the harbor area. On a clear day, of which they do not get many, it is a sight that can rejuvenate your soul.

I was nervous. A climb of this magnitude can be life or death. While I had the training on how to navigate my way through a glacier, it still seemed intimidating. I had already done Mt. Whitney twice, which happens to be the tallest mountain in the lower 48 states. I had also completed an ice climb in Alaska the year prior. Mt Rainier has an elevation of 14,411 feet just under Mt Whitney at 14,505. The difference will be the ice and dangers involved with the cold weather. As it turns out, there are 50-foot crevasses, sheer drops, and the ever-shifting ice, it was no ordinary challenge.

My first move was to hire a professional guide to help my chances of success. I had already been training for months in preparation of this physically demanding task. This was a three day hike up to the top and then down. Guides typically work in groups and bring climbers up the mountain in teams of two climbers to each guide. On day one you climb as a group before the guides separate everyone off into pairs. I am familiar with this process since I have climbed with this service before. Its at this time that I want to become friends with other strong climbers so that we can be seen as a team before officially be put together

While I was sizing up the other climbers, I became friends with an Army Ranger. I felt like I had hit the climbing partner jack-pot.

We were officially paired up together on day two. As the day progressed, we were able to climb to the second big portion of the climb. Right about now, we were literally camping on a glacier above which were massive ice boulders, ready to destroy anything and everything that may lay in their path. These had already rolled down the mountain a few days before we got there, as the guide explained with a smile on his face. On our way, we had to cross multiple crevasses, some as deep as a 10-storied building. The peak was hidden from our view up the steep side of the mountain, but the skies were crystal clear. On these types of climbs, its best to get to bed early since the summit push usually begins in the middle of the night. This ensures that you can bag the peak with plenty of daylight left to get all the way back to the bottom of the mountain. Furthermore, daylight ensures that the weather stays calm. There is nothing like trying to fall asleep at 6pm knowing that some ice boulders the size of a Volkswagen might roll over you while sleeping.

We started at 1am with nothing more than headlights and our visibility was just a couple of feet. Anything beyond that was just impossible to see. It was pitch dark. Several hours into the morning hours, the guide told us that we had to refuel and take a break. Right about now, the snickers in my pocket was calling my name. It's amazing how much fuel you burn on these steep climbs and what you need to replenish your energy.

We sat there long enough that the sun started coming out. I think the guide had this perfectly planned for us to enjoy the 360-degree view. It was awe-inspiring. Nothing compares to the sheer brilliance and beauty of nature that we were witnessing. Amidst all this beauty and nature's grandeur came a looming sense of fear and another one of nature's work. As daylight spread, it exposed thousands of feet of vertical drops waiting just over the edge for anyone that slips and falls. That was a one-way ticket to your demise. We knew we were high above the sea level, but seeing the sheer depth of these falls that we never really expected to find so close to us, was a surprise. It was like staring right into your death that was just inches away from you.

While I admired and respected nature, my army friend was having second thoughts about the entire summiting plan. I didn't know that. He was backing out of a climb because of the intimidation that had gripped him. It was here that my sense of coaching came into play. I knew I had to be the person to help him push through and climb the last few hours to summit the peak. After all, there was no point in putting your body through so much work just to turn away when you could literally see your destination ahead of you.

I realized that I was the one that had to regain his confidence while maintaining my composure. I felt nervous about the deal, but, it turned into strength and fortitude for my army ranger buddy. I knew I had to push him through because if he was to quit, everyone else would have to. It was as simple as that and that was not in my plans.

For the next few minutes, which seemed like eternity, I encouraged him to have faith in his training and ability. That we were there to achieve our goals and had been given all the tools to accomplish that. He quickly overcame his fear of the cliff and immediate surroundings after re-gaining his composure. I had encouraged him to visualize how things would look like from the top of the mountain, and that actually helped him regain the confidence he needed. An hour and a half later, we were on the summit.

When you focus on your strengths and work with one another, one can go through challenges and help each other to walk through tough situations. It was a great moment for me and one of the best goals I had achieved that year.

Allowing my buddy to visualize the view, to visualize himself in that position, was a major morale booster. What people don't understand is just how powerful visualizations can be. Just as the name of this chapter suggests, he believed he could do it, and he went on to do it. He just needed a bit of a nudge in the right direction.

Even I was visualizing how we would look at the top of the summit, holding our sign, high fives, hugging, and congratulating each other. I believed in the vision, and I knew we could go on and achieve that. Yes, I had my fears, but I had to either focus on my fears or the opportunity of conquering them that I eventually did.

I know that many might not be hoping to climb a mountain any time soon, but perhaps they may be dreaming of buying their dream car. Whatever model it may be, visualize yourself walking into the dealership. Picture what you are wearing for the big occasion, how it feels to sign the papers, shake the hands of the salesperson, and saying “I’ll take it.” Think and visualize yourself as you walk towards your very own car. Feel the door handle as you grip it, hear the sound of the door unlocking, and feel the cold yet inviting seat of the car as you step inside. Visualize as many details as you can. What you end up doing is creating confidence within you. The more you visualize this consistently, the more you start believing it will happen for you.

People lack the ability to have confidence in themselves. They don’t have much to believe in themselves, or at least that’s what they think. All they can hear is the negativity within them and around them. Others have nothing better to do than to tell us “This is never going to work,” and funnily enough, we believe them.

“Yeah! You’re probably right!”

No! They’re not right. If anything, they are limiting themselves through their limiting beliefs, and then they try and limit you as well. What you say inside your head ultimately comes out as your own truth.

"I'm always going to be overweight."
"I'll never be as successful as that guy."
"I can't be that good."
"This isn't for me because I don't deserve it."

The more you feed your mind with negativity, the more it manifests as your reality. You will always be overweight. You will always feel that you are unworthy and miss out on every single opportunity that comes your way.

The point I am trying to make here is that we need to be extremely careful of what we feed our brains. We must know what we say to ourselves because it can alter how we live our lives. In these little private conversations that we have with ourselves, we need to be mindful and careful not to say anything that is negative in nature. Private self-talk is more important than you can imagine. What you believe, what you say to yourself, and what you allow into your brain on a daily basis is exactly who you will become. Choose wisely.

In short, it all starts with yourself. As for when? There's no better time than now!

Chapter 2

Recognize Your Success and Strengths

Make no mistake, it is hard to recognize your strengths and weaknesses. It requires you to self-analyze. It is easier said than done. For this purpose, I always carry around with me a yellow notepad that helps me reflect on my day-to-day activity, it serves as a quick reminder of what I am supposed to do and helps me jot down anything that I believe was helpful for me.

Sometimes, I use that to write down what my strengths are. Based on such strengths, I also try and recognize any success that follows using those strengths, as a way to validate and confirm the entry. If you start doing the same, you may be in for a surprise because more often than not, that strength or success can be right in front of us. We just don't realize it.

The Competitive Sportsman

For a good part of my life, I have been an active and competitive athlete. I have taken part in wrestling matches and enjoyed every bit of the competition. Furthermore, I have taken part in off-road car races for professional car companies, such as Ford Motors. I am not what you would describe as a traditional sportsman, such as a basketball player, a baseball enthusiast, or any of that. As it turns out, I don't watch any sports on TV at all. Of course, you have Jack Canfield for that.

Quite a few years ago, I heard him speak. He was the co-author for *Chicken Soup for the Soul*, along with Mark Victor Hansen. He went on to say the following:

"The average person watches enough TV that they can get four master's degrees in any field of study they want."

WOW! I was blown away by that. It was such an eye-opener that I turned my TV off for 10 years and have never really turned it back on with a few exceptions. I don't watch sports, sitcoms, or even the news. It is odd for someone who is in their 50s. You would expect a person of my age to tune into the TV, complain about how the economy has messed up, and how the new guys are continuing to take away our jobs, but that's not me.

In the first chapter, I spoke about how we should be extremely careful of what we feed our brain, and how we should steer clear of the negativity that we usually find ourselves surrounded with. TV, for all intents and purposes, is the ultimate source of negativity. Since I know I can't be bothered to feed anything negative to myself, the choice was rather obvious. Either the TV goes, or my brain goes. I chose the former.

Not so long ago, I started a Tequila company called Azunia Tequila. This was in 2007. I was incredibly lucky to have great investors like Peter Jacobson from the PGA Tour, a pro-golfer. We also had Pat Kilkenny, another high net-worth individual as well as the past athletic director for Oregon. He was part of the origination of the Ducks and all the marketing they produced in that area.

One day, Pat came to me and told him how he was considering getting Bill Walton involved in the company. He wanted to know if this was something that would click with me. To be honest, I trusted Pat. He had a lot riding on this company, and so did I. If he thought Bill would be a good fit for the group, I was in. I was told that Bill is one of the best out there, and he is loved by many. Naturally, I looked him up on

Google because, embarrassingly enough, I didn't even know who he was.

Side note: Don't worry if you don't know who he is. He is rated as one of the best 100 basketball players of all time.

Bill Walton was also a very close friend of John Wooden, from UCLA, and was a part of the winning team when John Wooden was the coach. Of course, I had no idea, but after a few minutes of research I knew I was looking at a solid partner already.

The initial success we had was based on previous relationships and grinding away selling on the streets. The product sold itself once we got it into the hands of the buyers and consumers. However, we needed a small hook or edge on the competitors. Now that I think back about it, I realize how I was completely unaware of just how incredible of a person Bill Walton was.

Once, we went to the Staples Center to watch a game. Bill was accompanied by a few customers, his son, and I happened to be there too. His son was coaching at the time. It took some time to reach our seats because, unlike me, everyone knew who he was, and he ensured he spoke to everyone before arriving at the seating area. We sat down and had a great game to experience. Later, he introduced me to all the celebrities around us, including Jack Nicholson, who attends every single Lakers game. Jack asked me if Bill worked for me, and Bill answered that he did, which was just hilarious. He went on to say "I do whatever Jim tells me to do."

The game was over, and it was time to leave the arena. However, I was not at all expecting to witness and experience what was about to happen next. I knew I had strength, but it was about to show its full scale, and needless to say, I was completely taken by surprise. Most people know that Bill happens to be one of the most injured players of all time in basketball, and I didn't. Due to this fact, we had to leave a little bit early.

We walked across the backend of the court and started to walk up the stairs to take the way out. Just in the first five steps, Bill received a standing ovation from the entire west end of stadium, even though the game was still being played. Bleachers around us showed their respect for the legendary icon, and all I could do was to absorb that moment, feel the sheer energy levels that were tearing the roof apart, and be left in awe. I looked around, and everyone was clapping, cheering him on, and it was just bizarre. At that moment, I turned around towards my customer, who was also at the event with us, and I said "Wow! I have the right partner in this business."

That moment was what I needed because, at that moment alone, I learned just how incredible of a strength I had that I continued to discount since the start. I realized that sometimes, even the most obvious of strengths take time to manifest, but when they do, they hit you over the head, making you realize "Damn!" I had that moment right there.

The lesson here is simple. Your success and strengths may be there right in front of you, but it is always up to you to recognize what they are. Take the time out to dig them out, figure them out, learn them, and master them. Of course, you can't do it right now and say "Hey! I'm good with numbers." It is a process that requires consistency and time. You need to work on figuring out your true strengths and give it time every day.

In my case, I had a team member who was right under my nose, and I failed to identify and recognize his true potential and worth. It took a standing ovation for me to truly understand and appreciate just how incredible of strength and a person he was to me, and to pretty much anyone else he could have chosen to work with.

As leaders, we often have team members on our teams, and if we do not ask the right questions or provide the right amount of attention to figure them out for who they really are, we may end up missing out on a lot of opportunities. It is also possible that this team member may help you enter an arena that you may not have already looked at and, as an entrepreneur, it is just the kind of opportunity we are always looking for.

Realizing the strength in my team, we went on to leverage that to gain national exposure. We started doing public engagements through Q&As, both Bill and I and helped teach leadership skills to others. We went on to teach the importance of consistent pursuit by using our own experience and knowledge to educate people and help them grow as well.

It's All About the Perspective

It is human nature that the mind tends to initially jump towards the negative. If you were to be given an opportunity to make millions of dollars, the first thing that would come to mind would be "why me?" or "what's the catch?" Either that, or you would dismiss it thinking "it's just another scheme to rid me of my money." Such a perspective, such a mindset is what ensures we are overlooking the possible gains and true potential of the opportunity that is being presented to us.

We often try and look for the easy way out. We are always trying to figure out ways where we don't have to put in the efforts and jump straight to the results. The reason we do that is simply to accommodate our weaknesses. It all goes back to the internal dialogues that we have with ourselves. We are often chipping away on our own weaknesses instead of building ourselves up. The same is the case in businesses as well, and that ultimately leads to the downfall of a business.

Oftentimes, the person that is working the hardest is easily overlooked because they are the ones working the hardest. If we focus on our strengths and consider the successes that these people have contributed to, we can build upon those weaknesses as a unit, as a team.

To be honest, people lack confidence in themselves. They are far too interested in staying within their comfort zones. What they don't realize is that growth, success, and joy, all lie outside the comfort zone.

My mother has been a part of the Alcohol Anonymous (AA) program most of her life, and she is very proud of it, and so am I for her success. On several occasions, she has said to me:

"People sit in their shit because it's warm!"

It is a harsh reality and one that can be witnessed literally everywhere. We are far too accustomed to having life the way it is right now that we don't really put in the efforts to step outside the comfort zone and seek change. The more worrying thing is that people are okay with being comfortable. To be honest, it's time to get uncomfortable!

Smaller Wins Matter

Many people don't have the kind of professional success as a basketball player or an entrepreneur, and some may not have tasted success yet, but that's what makes everyone so unique. It is probably because they may not have tasted smaller victories when they were young. It could be because they didn't have a great sports coach at school or someone who could train them through the early stages of their professional career. When you take away these smaller wins, you take away the drive, the passion, and that force that propels you towards success.

As a coach, it is all about analyzing what people do have and then giving them the best opportunity to build upon. As a coach, I love it when I have clients who have professional sports or athletic backgrounds because it makes the entire transition a lot smoother. Similarly, if someone had a successful business run and they wish to transition into some other field, I simply analyze what this person has as their strengths, and what kind of successes they have experienced. This allows me to know what to use as a tool to help them move and transition into the new venture a lot easier.

Then, there are people who don't realize what their talents are. I am not saying that I do not serve them, but it only makes the process a bit longer because now, I have to go through everything they have, help them figure out and understand what their talents and strengths are, and then start working with them towards a better future. Pulling that information out of them is challenging at times. People who do not know what their talents are often do not have much success because they never really knew what skill or talent they should rely on to find said success.

Make no mistake; we all have talents. We all have some skills that we can bring to the table, and we all have something that we are extremely passionate about. There is not a soul on earth that can claim they have none. All it takes is some time to look inside and figure it out, and that is where the hard work comes in. As a coach, as a consultant, I look forward to these challenges because they can be the most rewarding ones. Knowing that you were able to help someone discover their passion, their skills, and their talents, and helping them achieve success is a reward that cannot be matched by any other experience.

Chapter 3

Values

It took me almost an entire lifetime to figure out just how important my values are. These relate to my happiness and where I choose to go in my life. Of course, I did know my values and I was able to figure them out successfully in the early parts of my life, but I never really got around to applying them properly. This means that I couldn't exactly lead the kind of life that I lead now, and that is simply because I did not prioritize my values or understand just how they can contribute to my success.

I did enjoy a very successful career at In N Out Burger. As I mentioned earlier, I ended up as the most successful store manager, selling 1 million burgers in a year. In terms of money, I was making a high six-figure income. Furthermore, my brother was steaming towards becoming the president of the company.

Side note: For anyone who doesn't know In N Out Burger, they only sell burgers and fries, with drinks. That's it!

For me, the work was boring and despite making the kind of money I was making, I was very unsatisfied. I wasn't satisfied because I knew I had a lot more to offer. I knew that I had more skills and talents that I felt were being wasted away. Although that was my lack of maturity looking back at it now.

Around the same time, I was in a downward spiral where all I could think about was making money as my marriage deteriorated. I was being very selfish with what I was earning and how I was using those earnings. To give you an idea, I took a very fancy snowboarding trip to Mammoth Mountain. I ended up spending $5,000. Many would claim that it is a trip of a lifetime, but for me, it was just another weekend.

I never realized just how selfish that trip was until the following weekend. This is where I went on a mission trip with Mariners Church group in Newport Beach. We were going to spend the day visiting a few Orphanages in Baja Mexico. There were around 20 of us, and there were 2 vans in total. The budget for the entire trip was also $5,000. That's 2 vans worth of people and enough supplies for at least 4 or 5 orphanages. Furthermore, those supplies would last some of those orphanages a couple of months.

Imagine how shocked I was when I realized just how selfishly I spent $5,000 in Mammoth on a single weekend. Seeing people give and receive, was a completely different experience. These orphanages were receiving food and supplies that would help them last for months to come, and while giving those to them, it was an experience that I couldn't explain in words.

When I got back home, I realized how I was living for the completely wrong reasons. Just 7 or 8 days ago, I ended up blowing $5,000 on myself, selfishly, whereas the very same $5,000 could have supported a couple of orphanages, dozens of kids, have enough supplies to last a month or two. That broke me apart inside. It was there that I decided to change how I lived my life.

No longer was I going to live for me. Instead, I chose to live for others. I decided to be the one to give back to the ones in need. Following that, I ended up quitting my very well-paying job, and my family wasn't exactly pleased with that decision. They were literally not talking to me for 2 years that followed because to them, I was being a fool for walking away from a career of a lifetime. They also recognized the downward spiral in my marriage and the trouble I was causing in my arrogance.

Facing my family's dismay and their anger, I decided to move as far away as possible. Turned out, I ended up at Lake Tahoe. At this point, I was willing to make minimum wage, which I did. Soon, I found a job where I was taking pictures of people at Kirkwood Ski Resort for tips. I didn't do this because I didn't have any other option, but I did this to reorganize who I was as a person.

Around this time, I was 28 years old. I realized that there is a lot more in life that I can go out, explore, and learn. Already, I had sold everything, moved away from my family, and moved to Lake Tahoe. As fate would have it, I had a DNA that dictated to me what I believed would be what I would go on to achieve. Just a month after, I ended up acquiring a second job as a buffet manager for Harvey's Casino. I gravitated there to what some would be a dream job, to become a VIP host. There, if I saw the gamblers throwing big money down on the Blackjack table, I would come in to tell them how I could offer them a free meal and a hotel room. I also hosted them for outdoor activities like hunting, fishing, boating, and more. That was my job.

The point of sharing this entire story isn't to win sympathy. It is to teach everyone just how critically important your values are, and how they can contribute towards your ultimate goals and success. Your core values help you identify the real you and who you can be. It was only recently that I was able to fully utilize my values to their maximum potential.

Of course, I did learn a big reason earlier in life, much earlier than most people do. I learned that I was living for all the wrong reasons. I don't want to take that away from myself. What I've done in the last three years, however, was completely different. A lot of this comes from my work with David Meltzer and him talking about values all the time. I am very proud to say and share what these values are:

1. God
2. Family
3. Health
4. Giving Back
5. Having time
6. Business

What's critical to note here is that making money is the last of my values. It is literally the least important thing for me. It may sound somewhat ironic, especially considering that I just came out of arguably the most prosperous 3 years of my life. It is simply because I center everything around these values.

Faith, above all, is the most important value for me, followed by my family. When I make decisions about what I am going to do, where I'm going, I always ensure that these decisions are in alignment with my values. This means that if the family is the second-most important thing in my life, next to God, I will align any decisions so that they will not affect my family dynamic. As an example, if I wanted to buy a really expensive car for myself at the expense of my family needing something or spending extra time with my family on a holiday, taking them to places and having quality time together, my values are out of order if I buy the vehicle.

That's just a simple example. Almost every single day, we entrepreneurs are faced with a barrage of decisions that we have to make. Instead of being impulsive, we choose to ensure we know our values, keep them in our mind, analyze the decision and see if that decision falls in line with these values. If yes is the answer, we go for it, but if something isn't lining up, it's a solid no.

If taking a job out of state meant that I would end up making half a million dollars more than I am making right now, I would not do it. The reason is simple because making money is my last priority, and my family comes well above that. I cannot leave my family here and rush towards another state to take on a job that pays me more. That's going directly against my core values, and that, to me, would be a poor decision to leave and chase a job.

To me, values are significantly critical. Whether you are a business professional, an entrepreneur, or even an employee that works 9 to 5, know what your values are and center all your life's decisions around your values. Perhaps now, it would make sense to you why I decided to quit that job and restart my entire life from Lake Tahoe at minimum wage.

It was the change of environment that did it for me, and quite often, that is all you need in order to get your priorities and values straight. However, there still remains one big misconception that needs to be addressed.

An alarming number of people, by which I mean the majority of them, consider financial success for happiness. It is a common theme, and regardless of how many times I repeat and reiterate the fact that money cannot buy happiness, people still continue to believe otherwise. To me, it was as black and white as it got. I was already making a high six-figure salary, that too when I was in my mid-20s. This is unheard of even in times like today. I was doing that back in the 80s. However, no amount of money that I was making made me feel happy, fulfilled, or anything close.

Don't get me wrong because I am not one of those who claim that money is the root of all evil. We need it, whether you like it or not, to do quite a lot of things in life. With money, we can help others, and one of my values happens to give people something back. Making money is what allows me to provide for my family, to give back the community and those who really need the support. It is what helps me to buy myself more time. However, money, at no point in time, helps me buy happiness.

Clear Values, Lesser Problems

There are many people who continue to struggle in their day-to-day lives, and that is because they are either not taking the time to figure out what their values are, or they know them and are otherwise ignoring their importance. Either way, you are setting yourself up for failure or lack of fulfillment in life.

When you know your values, and prioritize them accordingly, everything in life becomes far easier. No longer will you be spending hours and days to come to a decision. No longer will you need to seek feedback from everyone around you. Knowing your values, you can gauge the opportunity, figure out if it is in alignment with your values, and either go for it or turn it down.

Those who have no idea of what their values are going to struggle while making even the easiest of decisions. They would experience restlessness throughout the night and anxiety throughout the day. The inability to make a decision while time continues to tick away will only go on to affect you mentally and emotionally. In most cases, you would end up making a decision based on your emotions, and such decisions are the leading causes of downfall, depression, stress, anxiety, and even death at times.

When you have a clear set of values, you have certainty with you. It is said that a person with certainty is a dangerous person, and that is because they know exactly what they want, and how they are going to move forward. There is literally nothing that can shake them off their path because they know their values, and they know what they need to do in order to move forward.

We are the product of not only what we have within us, but we are also a product of the people we surround ourselves with. If we know our values, and we know that our friends are in alignment with our values, we will certainly have a strong bond to share. However, if we end up with a social circle that does not match our values, we will struggle to maintain a healthy conversation, feel left out, and will eventually leave.

To give you an example, since my family is my second most important value, I would rather spend my time with other families, people who spend time with their children and spouses as opposed to friends who have nothing better to do than to hit the bar on a Saturday and drink their minds out. The latter neither aligns with my values nor is it something that I would consider as time well spent. Of course, we can still be friends and spend time doing something that fits both of our values at a different time.

It's okay to cut the draggers from your life because they will bring you down from your values or force you to overlook the importance of your values. For anyone who wishes to learn something that will serve them throughout their lives, figure out what your priorities are, write them down on a piece of paper, and then prioritize them. The final shape of that list is what must reflect what you believe in and truly stand for. There are no right or wrong values here because each one of us is unique and different. It is possible that someone out there may not prioritize faith at the top, or perhaps there may be those who want to prioritize adventure over others. Whatever these may be, write them down and learn about them.

Sticking to your values may not always come easy. For me as I removed my thirst for making money, I gained the desire to have a family. I had been improving my life with God but still felt a major hole in my heart. My wife at the time had decided that kids were not important to her anymore. To be honest, our marriage had declined to a point where that was a good decision in hindsight. I would not have wanted kids with me either. Because I was a person of faith, I struggled to pursue the "divorce" option and continued down a path of two lives moving further and further apart over time. In the end, having kids and being a father was not something I was willing to miss in life. I eventually separated from a wife of 19 years after sabotaging anything good that had remained. I needed a good dose of re-visiting my values and who I was. I took a major detour in life post-divorce when God finally had enough. He was gracious enough to put an amazing woman in my life that helped me become everything I am today. If I did not understand my own values, I would not have realized how perfect things would become.

Typically, if someone was looking to start a business, for anyone to work with me, I made it a requirement for that person to write down a business plan. It would be through this business plan that I can learn more about the business and get to know just how serious the person is. However, before all that, I want my clients to assign their own personal values first before moving on to the business phase. That's just how important values are for me.

Quite often, your business plan will pull you away from your values. For example, if you are a man of faith, and you end up starting a gambling business online, you would find yourself struggling because your faith, in most cases, would simply not allow you to gamble or be a part of anything related to gambling. Your business, therefore, must align with your values, not the other way around.

Chapter 4

Faith Over Fear

"Faith over fear!"

David Meltzer

This, as a statement, became a pivotal for me after I learned my values and centered my life around them. I realized just how important it was to have God and faith in my life. Knowing that God was always there for me, always provided for me, and was always there when I needed help, guidance, and direction was more powerful than any other feeling I knew. God made us perfect, we mess things up.

I never really gave Him that much credit for all I had achieved, but when I look back at my In N Out Burger career, it was a Christian organization based purely on Christian beliefs. You can look at the bottom of the burger bag, the French fry tray, the T-shirt, and the cups, you will find scripture on each of them.

I realize that God has been a part of my life ever since I was 6 years old. I was of the firm belief that He was there for me. However, I never really appreciated the importance of my faith in him until I was older. Allowing myself to have faith over any fear was the real challenge because it is quite easy to succumb to what society may say, what others around you may say, and bow in the face of fear. Almost anyone can do that, but what most can't do is to stand their ground, have an unshakable belief that God will see them through, help them walk right past those frightening situations victorious. Give Faith a chance and see what happens, God might just surprise you.

Taking a Leap of Faith

Later, I decided to view my values and priorities in order and come up with an image of a business that they would fit in. When you identify a set of values, you can start with a vague idea of what you want to do, but with a bit more time and thinking, you can come to a clearer picture of what your business would look like, what it would do, and how it would function. When I put my values in place, consultancy seemed the most obvious choice. However, it was a completely new realm for me. I had never done that before, and this is where I needed all the faith, I had to help conquer my fear.

The business I envisioned had a few key characteristics:

1. I wanted to work from home.
2. I wanted to make a high six-figure income to replace the income I was already making at the tequila business I had started.
3. I needed the faith to help me walk away from a place of security where I had big investors and a guaranteed salary.
4. Lastly, I wanted to pick my family up and move into an environment that would be conducive to the life we wanted to live.

I had already investigated relocating and the only two options I came up with were Montana or Texas. Choosing between the two, was a lot easier than I thought initially because we fell in love with Montana almost immediately. We knew we wanted to settle there, and have a ranch for ourselves.

I wanted to do all of this while having faith that my idea to establish a consultancy business would be the right one, and that I would make things work despite the growing fears that lingered within me. There were so many questions, so many "what ifs" that continued to plague my mind, but it was faith over these petty fears that helped me push through and get started with a business that was perfectly in line with my core values. This was my big "Yes".

When you try to pull something out of nothing, it can often be challenging and intimidating. I was never a consultant, had never even tried to be one before any of this. Since I loved helping people, I was always the go-to guy for many to seek advice from, and I would always be happy to share my opinions with people. Finally, a consultant requires a role of authority, and as it turned out, I was always in charge of something throughout my wide range of professional experiences.

"We've paid the dummy tax so somebody else doesn't have to!"

Dave Meltzer

All I had to do now was to go out on a limb; I wound up giving away consulting for 6 months, while still being in the comfort of my home before we moved to Montana. This was necessary for me to get my eye into the business, understand what it feels like and how things would work for me. I already had a job, but I took the time out to ensure I could also pay attention to this new business as well.

The more I consulted and coached, the more faith I started developing in the process. Soon enough, I gained enough confidence to know that I could, in fact, become a good consultant and that I would be able to replace the income I was already making. Besides, I love giving, and if you know the laws of attraction, the more I gave away, the more I ended up receiving.

Giving is another concept that people don't understand. Giving something away and giving it away with no expectations in return are two quite different things. In the former, you are normally providing something to someone, hoping that they would lend you a favor in return. I preferred the latter where I gave to people and never expected anything in return. The more you give, the more will come back to you, and that is not just with finances. It could be finding new friends, a more comfortable life, some form of good news, or even a brand-new opportunity.

Faith Overshadows Fear

When you have greater faith than your fears, you will receive the rewards for that. You can encounter fear in all shapes and sizes. Here are some of the more common ones:

- Fear of rejection

- Fear of failure
- Fear of missing out (FOMO)
- Fear of the unknown
- Fear of losing what you may have

Most people who want to become an entrepreneur, start their own business, or do something other than a regular 9 to 5 job, may face the fear of rejection. They are far too worried about the fact that their immediate social circle, such as their friends, peers, and sometimes the family members as well, will reject their ideas and, ultimately, reject them. This is arguably the most common fear almost every entrepreneur today has gone through.

Fortunately, I never had the fear of rejection. My mantra was always "What you believe is what you will achieve," and I have always followed that. I didn't care what people thought about me or if they believed in what I was doing. I stayed true to my beliefs. However, this doesn't mean that I didn't have any fears at all. As it turns out, I did.

I was concerned by the idea of not being able to replace my income. Jumping ships might have been easier if I was single, but now, I was a father, a husband, and the provider for the house. All the responsibilities fell on my shoulders. I am fortunate because I have the type of wife that would jump in and work as hard as she had to in support of my plan. She would never back down in a time of need. Being in the position that I was in, my fear came from the financial perspective, meaning that I was afraid of the idea of not making enough money to support my family, pay those bills, and taxes. It took some time, and it was no ordinary feat for me to step out on my own, walk out of the umbrella that I was already under, and find the faith to help me see myself all the way through to my perceived destination. It was faith that I leaned on, relied upon, and counted on to get me through and ensure that all the bills would be paid, there would be food on the table, that we would have a beautiful place to live in, and that neither me nor my family would have to worry about how we would be able to meet any additional expenses. I had faith that I would be able to do all of that without actually changing my lifestyle. Furthermore, I believed that if I could make it in one area, I would do the same in another area too. This went both ways:

1. If I could be a success in this area, that meant I could be successful in another area.
2. If I could make half a million dollars in this area, I could make the same in other areas as well.

Overcoming My Fears

Just how did I overcome my fears? As I transitioned into my consulting business, I started to make some money.

At the same time, I started listening to Gary V. If you haven't heard him before, he is a great marketing influencer. One thing he always talks about is how nobody should be broke. He talks about how anyone can go on Craigslist and browse the section that reads "For Free" to get something there from any area.

He quoted an example of how one person went on to pick up a sofa for free, got it back using the subway, and sold that in their hometown for $20. The example he uses is to reinforces the idea of how there is absolutely no reason why anyone shouldn't have any money. Be creative!

I took that advice literally and decided to make as much money as I could. I was already facing the fear of not having enough money to make the transition. Sure enough, I found myself in the garage and I decided to go through the things that I could sell at the pawnshop. The funny thing is that I had never been to a pawn shop so I had absolutely no idea what a pawn shop would even buy. Despite that, I wanted to get ahead of the game and do what was needed to make some money.

This may not be the perfect display of faith, but it did prove that you can make money if you had a goal. I wouldn't deny the fact that I had a lot of fun selling some old speakers, posters, and some of the most random things a pawn shop would buy. In the process, I also developed a good relationship with the pawnshop.

I didn't stop at the pawnshop either. I learned that we had a local swap meet on Sundays where I could really move a lot of stuff. After raiding my old race shop, I had a truckload of car parts and auto supplies. This netted $1000's of dollars to add to the stash I was collecting. Of course, Gary was right that anyone could walk away with $20 in their pocket if they are smart enough and willing to get out there and do the work. As much fun as I was having, I decided to lean on my faith more. Just recently, I completed my third successful year as a consulting professional.

Shifting the Mindset

Faith isn't that you put your faith in God and don't lift a finger. You need to do your part as well, and a major part of that is acquiring the right mindset.

Most people say that they have complete faith in God and that they worked all they could and still didn't end up with the kind of results they expected. The reason for that is simple. While you might have done everything right, your mindset might have been the one that operated from the place of scarcity.

A scarcity mindset pushes you to assume you don't have enough of something, whether it is money, health, time, opportunities, clients, sales, or anything else. If you believe you do not have enough money or worry that you may not be able to make enough to pay the bills, you will actually run into the very same reality. On the other hand, if you are someone who operates from a place of abundance, everything changes.

Faith plays a vital part in helping you find the right mindset. If you have faith in God, or a higher power, or the universe, and you believe that you will be provided for, taken care of, and be guided in case you run into problems, you will be able to rest yourself assured that you have all you need to get started and that you will go on to find significant success.

For example, there are two types of people, both of whom are asked to walk through a ball of fire. One believes that God will help him walk through it and that he will be okay because he has all the skills and strength he needs to get the job done. On the other hand, the other person thinks about how much it would hurt or what would happen if something was to go wrong. That is a sign that shows a lack of faith and a scarcity mindset. In this case, the first one will most likely end up walking through the challenge while the other would either back out or be injured in the process.

You need faith to walk through a challenge, and you need the right mindset to help you realize that you have what it takes to get the job done. Similarly, if you want to start a business, you need this same mindset to gain a competitive advantage over others.

By having faith, we can overcome many more obstacles than others. We know how the story ends because God will take care of all of us in everything we do. If you live with that faith, that belief, and that mindset, not only will you find yourself more satisfied as a person, as an employee, and an entrepreneur, but you would also be able to overcome things that you would have never thought you could. In the end, you will be far stronger for those adversities, and you will overcome each one of them.

When I first started consulting, it was always about finding one client, spending a month, getting the job done, and then finding another one. The process would repeat itself. Every single time, for the last 36 months, God has provided me with yet another opportunity on His time, not mine, to meet my needs. It was because I had immense faith in Him. I gave back to people, without questions, without any expectations of getting something in return, and that's where I found more people coming to me.

If giving back is a part of who you are, is one of your core values, you will find opportunities the likes of which may not appear elsewhere. Even if you are writing a check for the last few dollars you have in your bank account with the intention of giving it to someone, to help them, just because you have faith that it will come back to you, you will be provided for with far more.

In the last 36 months, there have been weeks where I have gone wondering "Where is this going to come from?" And every single time, another opportunity has come to my doorstep at the right moment and at the right time. I have never regretted a single decision that I made.

You don't have to be of a particular faith or religion to have faith. You can still go on to develop faith in the process. However, if you can believe in the faith that He promises us, then you will see the rewards. That is the basis of Christianity. Without believing that He exists, virtually no religion is complete, no faith is complete. When you put faith in Him, He repays you in a mysterious yet rewarding way as a thank you and a reminder that He has faith in you to get the job done and do the right thing.

When you place the finances, the family, the business, and everything else in His hands, He will provide.

Chapter 5

Be Grateful

Being privileged enough to live within the United States of America, we often take things for granted. What we should really be doing is place ourselves in a position of gratitude for what we have been given. People across the world wish to come to the US, settle down, have a family, and seek opportunities that no other country on earth can offer, and yet, here we are taking things for granted and missing out on so much in life, and that is indicative of lack of gratitude in our lives.

I walk all of my clients, whether business clients or life-coaching clients, through the exercise of gratitude. Of course, I am not reinventing the wheel here. All I am doing is reinforcing what others before me have said on numerous occasions throughout history. There is no greater tool that costs you nothing than the gift of gratitude. Just look around you and realize how much you have to be grateful for. You have a roof over your head, food on the table, a book to read on a smartphone or some electronic device. You have the freedom to roam around where you want to, have a job that pays you, or a business that you are operating. The list could go on forever.

I ask all my clients to wake up in the morning and write down 5 things they are grateful for. If you are really good at it, you would do this before you go to bed as well. The exercise is daily, and that means by the end of the first month, you would have 150 things, at minimum, to be grateful for. What's more interesting is that in the times that we live in currently, we have Americans who are stuck in foreign lands. Even if they want to, they can't get out due to restrictions or other problems. They would be grateful for a safe roof over their head where they would not be fearful of someone knocking on their door in the morning, ready to take them away.

To say that I am grateful for a warm bed, a cozy roof over my head, for the meals that are served on the table, a business model that allows me to succeed, and the fact that I am a proud resident of the US, it's neither obnoxious nor ridiculous. The fact of the matter is that I am truly grateful that God chose to provide me all of this and more. When I have clients who find themselves stumped, not knowing what they feel grateful for, I remind them to start with the roof that they have over their head, the meal that awaits them in the refrigerator, and their ability to walk, talk, see, hear, and speak.

There is a lot more to be grateful for than you might imagine. If you can start your day with being grateful, if you can spend the first 15 minutes of your morning going through the things that you are grateful for and writing them down, the first oppositions you meet that day will be met with a sense of gratitude. It will take a significantly longer time for anything to chip away from your gratitude. If you are grateful, you fill up on positivity, and that positivity is what ensures that you have a great day ahead.

If you are grateful first thing in the morning, and you make it to your breakfast table and your kid comes in, which causes a ruckus, you wouldn't feel bad at all. Why? Because you probably already started your morning by being grateful that you have a child. The perspective changes and now you gain more tolerance as well. You start viewing the very same activity as pleasurable and something to be thankful for instead of being annoyed by it.

I have watched my kids, who are 6 and 8 now, grow as humans, and I have heard them say some of the most precious and meaningful things before bed. We instituted a mandatory "name 3 things you are grateful for" every night before bedtime the entire last year. Of course, they are young, and that means that they come up with some of the most honest and sweet things they find themselves grateful for.

When you really listen to those naïve minds and the things they say, you would hear things like:

- I'm grateful for mommy and daddy
- I'm grateful for my friends
- I'm grateful for the dinner we had tonight
- I'm grateful for mommy not having to go to work
- I'm grateful for daddy driving us to school

That has an effect on you. It resonates with you and shows you what is truly important in life, and what your real values are.

The Effects of Gratitude

If you can identify gratitude in your business, and what you have in business, you will find success much faster and easier. I am consulting with a restaurant business currently. It has two stores. As a nation, we know how there is an acute shortage of employees almost everywhere. However, this particular restaurant owner was attacked by some media that felt like he wasn't running his business to the degree that he had advertised. Throughout my coaching sessions, he spoke about all the negative things that were said about him, his wife, his business, and how he operated.

Each of these sessions was held in one of the dining rooms of his restaurant. The exercise would literally repeat and he would discuss something new and more negative than the previous session that he heard over the news or through someone else, and it was going nowhere. I eventually stepped in and made it clear that we will no longer dwell in the past. What was done was done.

Every single time that I sat in that restaurant, listening to him talking about his past and all the negative things he would share, I witnessed his dining room fill with people to their capacity. I saw his team serve each customer with an honest smile, and I watched his staff grow. This also showed me that he had enough team members that could handle all operations. Naturally, I highlighted all of that for him and told him how he was not being grateful for what he already has. While he complained about his past, I saw a clear lack of gratitude for how incredible his business was operating, even in tougher times where people were literally trying to make a living elsewhere. Because this person was not open to the gratitude, to the gifts that God sent to him, things weren't going well for him.

Everything he wanted, was right in front of him, and I didn't hesitate to tell him that. I showed him how to count his blessings and start exercising gratitude, with a focus on whatever was going on within his business. There was a bigger picture at play here, and it was my job to show him that.

One of his complaints was that his other restaurant wasn't doing very well as it was suffering the consequences of the negative media attacks.

"Let me ask you an honest question. If your other restaurant was as successful as this one, would you be able to handle the business? Do you have enough staff down there?"

"Not really. The staff at the other location is required to bake fresh bread and prep food items needed for both stores. They are swamped now with the business we have."

Even his perceived failure of the other restaurant, was playing a part that he should be grateful for because it continued to ensure the success of this restaurant. I told him how if the other restaurant was to get busy, he wouldn't be able to continue his operations in this restaurant smoothly, and it would eventually collapse.

"You know what, Jim? You're right!"

In business, we have so much that happens for us, but it is human nature that we try to focus on what we want or don't have as opposed to being grateful for what we have.

When we change our mindset, change our perspective, we would not only learn how to be more grateful, but we would actually attract a lot more success in return as a reward.

Don't Give Up

Unfortunately, I have been through a divorce. It was a difficult time because I literally gave up. I've learned that giving up is not an option, it never should have been. This is particularly true if you are in a life-long commitment. Because of this failure, I am a major proponent of working through challenges that life may throw my way while having faith in the commitments I make. Similarly, I have encouraged many others to do the same. Their relationships, their long-term commitments, are worth the fight. All we need to do is to stick through the tougher part.

There is no denying that there is negativity spreading across the globe right now, whether in the form of a disease, financial or economic crunch. Due to this negativity being everywhere, it is easy for people to succumb to it. One of the best ways to get rid of negativity is to live by the principle of gratitude. Using the very same exercise that I tell my clients;

you can find yourself transforming into this positive being that cannot be slowed down by any negativity out there.

I have made it a point in my life to follow and practice gratitude, and for good reasons too. Even when adversities come my way, I am thankful that they do, and that is because it allows me a chance to grow as a person, as a businessman, and as a coach. Through these tiny hiccups in life, we learn a lot about what we might have done wrong and realize that despite the bad, we still have a lot left to be thankful for in life and in business.

Just a few mornings ago, I had a cup of coffee with an established author, Rod Kuntz. He is currently running for City Council and has published a brilliant book *The W.A.R.P.A.T.H. Alliance*. He lives a life of gratitude, and he loves giving back to people. We actually met only because we shared common beliefs and perspectives on things, such as my love to give back to people and my way of practicing gratitude. While the meeting was only 1.5 hours long, we shared a lot of our common interests and really got to know each other better. When you are grateful in life, you can attract others who may be following the same pattern, the same concepts, and have the same mindset as you. These are the people who are preoccupied with giving, as opposed to having their hands out or telling the world what they are interested in. If there is anything that you need to become a successful person, it is to surround yourself with people like Rod, people who love to give.

If we don't have money, one might think that we cannot have the ability to give at all. However, there is always a way to go about that. Through some of the stories and events I have shared with you, it is evident that there is more to give to the world than just money and financial assistance. It can be knowledge, advice, experience, emotional support, help, your time, and any other kind of assistance.

The more you start focusing on others, the more you realize just how much you are already blessed with. While many would complain about the fact that they may not have a well-paying job, or that their business isn't doing as good, it is better to change perspectives and think about those who may not have a job or a business at all. Almost immediately, everything changes. From there, you can then decide how they can be of value to others, and that is essentially the difference between those who become successful and those who dream about success but end up with no results.

Chapter 6

Wear Your Blinders

I have been surfing since I was 13 years old. It was a sport of passion and something I did at least 5 days a week. Some of my best memories have to do with time spent in the ocean. My best friend Phil of many years would grab me before work, and we would hit the secret breaks of Palos Verdes or the isolated beaches down in Baja. We used to laugh when friends would ask us how it was, because our answer would always be “it was the best day ever”. When we would finally make it to work, on time, our hair would be sandy, and our noses dripped with salt water. We were living our best life. I have often said that Surfers make better CEO’s. That is due to our ability to make quick decisions and live with the consequences. You don’t jump on a big wave and second guess what you’re going to do. Give all you have, enjoy the ride, or crash and burn and deal with the consequences. But you always get back on the next wave.

At least 20 years ago, I was out surfing, enjoying a picturesque morning at the cliffs in Huntington Beach, California. When I got back to my car, I received a call of desperation to attend the Pacific Symphony Opera's Black-Tie affair. It was almost comical to think that I needed to go find a tuxedo while I was standing there wet, sandy, and wrapped in only a towel on Pacific Coast Highway. Despite the unusual circumstances, I managed to grab hold of a tuxedo for the evening, and I arrived just in time.

My ticket had me seated at the vendor's table next to Bill Eldien and Carl Nolet, the owners, and presidents of Ketel One Vodka. I sat down, and we started getting to know each other while having apple martinis. Soon after, Bill said:

"Jim, I really like your style. Would you be interested in working for us?"

"Bill. We are all dressed in the same black and white tuxedo drinking your martinis, of course, you like my style" I quipped.

He laughed a little and then insisted that we meet up on Monday and discuss how I could work for the team. Make no mistake; I said "YES" to this opportunity as it was a great honor to work for Ketel One Vodka that led to a wonderful ten-year career.

During my time there, I learned that we, meaning the company and I, were just small fish in a massive pond of vodka companies. At the time, Smirnoff Vodka happened to be the biggest domestic vodkas in the world, Absolut Vodka was selling north of 3 million cases every year, and we were barely making over 100,000 cases a year. Our goal was just to sell 1% of what these big guns were selling in the market.

It was there that I learned to put our blinders on. We lived with our story about the history of Ketel One, who we were, what we represented as a company and as a team, had faith in the quality of the bottle and the contents within, and we never worried about what other brands were doing. All we were worried about was delivering our story and what we stood for. This is where I learned the importance of having your blinders on, just like a racehorse on the track.

Stop Looking Around

Often, I am approached by entrepreneurs who want to dive into a business field that is saturated, such as the tequila industry, and they are extremely concerned about the competitiveness that they may experience. My first comment, which always happens to be the same, is:

"What are your values? What is your business plan? Why do you want to be in this business? What's important to you?"

I ask these questions to fully understand what is it that you are trying to achieve, and if it is something that you are prepared to do. Whatever may be true and right in your mind, we can operate with blinders on because it literally doesn't matter what other companies may be doing. All that matters is that you have an authentic story and are passionate about what you are doing. If you put in the time, you will be a success. The consistent pursuit will lead to success.

Often times, when you put those blinders on, it also means that you have to be patient, be persistent, and be consistent. By putting on the blinders, you are ignoring that external factor that may otherwise keep others pressurized and stressed. I am not saying that you completely cut yourself off from your surroundings, but by putting on blinders, you are effectively choosing to only learn the trend that may help you, nothing more, nothing less.

People get caught up in what their competitors may be doing, and that only leads to devastation and failure. This is because when you pay too much attention to your competition, you start changing things around to ensure you do whatever seems to be working for them, and the instance this change comes in, you find yourself derailed from your own goals and values. When you lose your values, you lose your purpose, and when you lose your purpose, you end up getting nowhere.

It is just like putting the blinders on a racehorse like I mentioned earlier. It cannot see what goes around it, and all it can do is to look dead straight and aim for the finish line to win the race. Similarly, putting on blinders means you are aiming straight to that revenue target you want to achieve, aiming straight for the finish line towards your goal, and generating sales that will provide you significant returns. It is not possible to do any of that by comparing yourself to others.

This is also true in competitive sports as I learned as an athlete in the Spartan Obstacle Racing Series. I was fortunate enough to have an incredible coach as I competed for four years before Covid shut things down. Coach Jordan taught me to race against my own time and ability while not worrying about the other racers. If I gave it everything I had to give and trained for, what more could I offer. It certainly did not matter where others were on the course since I was operating at 100% effort. Jordan would remind me:

“Jim! Don’t look behind you. It really doesn’t matter what they are doing. If you are doing the best job possible, doing what I have trained you to do, and you are running a six-and-a-half-minute mile, there is absolutely no point in looking behind you then.”

He explained how if someone better would pass me, meaning that I didn't have to waste my time looking anywhere else, just keep a laser focus on what lay ahead of me. My coach also pointed out the fact that no one knows who would show up to the race. It could be a bunch of beginners or professionals, and it still wouldn't matter. What I needed to know and control was my own ability, to ensure that I put my best out there till the end.

In competitive sports, I learned to put my blinders on and avoid peaking over my shoulder to see what or who was coming behind me, and just focus straight on the goal. If I was to look behind and see someone approaching me, they would immediately get into my head. This would cause me to be distracted and that could eventually lead me to lose focus and make an error in judgment.

I have followed the same principle in business ever since. With my blinders on, I have never looked around or behind me to see what's going on, who may be running towards me. Instead, I have always had my goals insight, and I have given my best every single day.

Be yourself. There is no reason for you be someone that you are not. Focus on your plan otherwise it may cause two problems:

1. The originator and the creator of the idea would have come up with the idea based on their own set

of values, and there is a good chance they may not be the kind of values you would have in place for your business. This can cause a clash of interests, and it will ultimately derail you completely from your own path and goals.

2. It takes away authenticity from your brand, your firm, and your reputation. The era we live in now is full of information, meaning you can develop your own thoughts and ideas based on principles that fit your business.

Be Authentic

Just like In n Out Burger, base your business purely on an authentic story. Authenticity has never mattered as much as it does today, and we have the internet to thank for that.

Today, the internet is awash with stories where fabricated realities are presented to lure the audience in and wow them. However, on the other side of the lens, things are very different. You may come across someone who is claiming to have the fanciest cars, the most luxurious house, and stating that they would let you in on the secret of how they got there, just to tempt the audience to buy the membership. Once you do, in most cases, you end up learning exactly what you already knew, or worse sometimes it turns out to be a scam altogether. This means that people will fall for such scams, lose trust in almost every single business that is listed on the internet, and that would be that. If, however, you have an authentic business, you stand a chance to be noticed, to be viewed, to be clicked, and to garner the attention of the masses.

In order to stand a chance and gain success, you must always base your business around the set of principles and values that you follow. Be authentic, be yourself, and be true to who you are. Everyone has a story to tell, and that means you don't really need to worry about fabricating anything. This is particularly important if you are hoping to start a business and provide investment opportunities to investors. If the investor sees the authenticity, they will invest, period.

People invest in people, not what they are selling or the kind of business they may have. Remember, if your business is based around your values, your business is essentially reflecting you, giving a fair idea to the investors of who you are as a person.

It has become a requirement for me to go through people's personal values and assigning them, building a business plan, having a Performa, and have some statistics that show the return on investment (ROI), but despite all that, I can guarantee that 9 out of 10 people still invest in people, not what the papers say about the business. If your business plan, the story behind it, can showcase an authentic story, show that you are passionate about what you plan to do, they will invest in you.

In the last 10 years, I have raised over 12 million dollars based on who I was, my grit, determination, and my passion for the company that I started. Of course, I did do the paperwork, meaning I drafted the business plan, created a Performa, and highlighted the ROI figures, but the people who chose to invest in my business stated that they invested because of me.

If you can find an investor who is willing to invest in you as a person, it would be a far better relationship because they would understand what you value and what is important to you. A business will succeed if it is based around values, principles, not just a Performa.

It is very important to look at the long-term objectives of your company as it relates to authenticity and standing true to that. Ketel One Vodka was built on 16 generations of father-to-son history. Over 319 years of history were already there when I started. That company was based purely on those values and was created here in Holland. Ultimately, the family made the decision to sell the distribution rights to Diageo, the largest spirit supplier on earth. Now, the brand had become more of a household name without a story of generations that went into making this company what it is today. Of course, the story still remained in the background, but the spotlight was now taken by the story in the foreground, and that belonged to

Diageo and their sales tactics. They went on to advertise the product through their traditional methods, including discounts, and typical industry promotions, and all of that was ordinary for them, but for the family, this was never done before. With time, the brand moved further away from that authenticity, and the relationship with the consumers was affected.

There is no denying that they continued to see success, but this time around, the success was more monetary, and with that, they lost the value of their authenticity. In the meantime, you have a small vodka brand in Texas named Tito's Vodka. These people are focusing on their original humble beginnings, while making domestic vodka. The founder, Bert "Tito" Beveridge, had the authenticity that he continues to promote today, and even though this brand has been around for 20 years, much younger than Ketel One, it has become one of the largest vodka companies in the World. The reason this company made it big is that they stayed true to their story.

What people fail to understand is that their story "IS" their competitive advantage. People want to know that you are really just like them. What you do may not matter to them as much as who you are as an individual, whether you are someone they can talk to, trust, and confide in. It is all about your values to determine what side of the fence you are on.

I am extremely proud that I am a citizen of the United States. The opportunities that we have here, to be a patriot, to serve the country, are things that resonate with my clients because I genuinely believe it is nothing short of a gift that God has bestowed upon me, upon us, in the United States.

Chapter 7

Goals – Write Them Down

"Everyone makes resolutions. Winners make lists of shit they are gonna do."

Andy Frisella

I have written down my goals throughout my life. For some, it could be as simple as writing them down on a notepad, a whiteboard, post-it notes, or even on their cell phones. Writing down your goals is arguably the most important lesson to learn here.

"But Jim, why should we write our goals?"

There is actual science involved here. While I won't complicate things by diving into how our brain works and present the ridiculously confusing terminologies, I will, however, present a much easier version of the same concept for you to digest.

Imagine you are tasked to get groceries. What is the first thing that you do? You write down a grocery list and all the items that you need.

"But I do groceries all the time. I don't need to write them down."

Those who don't may very well try, but they would always end up buying more than what they need, or end up coming back home and realize "Damn! I forgot to pick up bread." As a rule, You may never get everything that your needed. It is usually more or less, and that's a fact.

On the other hand, if you have a list with you, you will walk into the store and come out of it with exactly what you need. Yes, you can still buy more in case you figure out something was missing from the list, but that only happens if you had the original list, to begin with.

Goals work the very same way. When we write down our goals, they are there for us to remind ourselves what we need to focus on, what we need to achieve, and what we need to replace or change. If you don't write down your goals, the chances of achieving these goals are small, and that's yet another fact for you to digest.

Writing down goals brings them to life. If you have already gone through the values exercise from earlier, you will be able to establish what your goals are based on those values. Furthermore, if you are living your life authentically, you will achieve your goals.

It isn't necessarily on your time because, at the end of the day, it is always on God's time. However, you still have a role to play, and that is to put in the work required to achieve these goals. And part of the work is to write them down.

Our mind can easily be distracted during something important, and this also goes well with our goals. We may be aiming to achieve some kind of a goal, but somewhere in the middle, we may end up distracted. When that happens, it is easy to find ourselves deviating from the goal or losing track of it completely. As a result, we end up with the kind of results we never really wanted.

Goals can not only be achieved, but they can come full circle in life.

I met David Meltzer through a mutual friend. I had a publicist drive SEO traffic to my new beer and wine business that was purely based on online sales. I was told that SEO was incredibly important to grow my business. I was also told that a podcast was another great tool if I wanted SEO traffic. I could either start my own or I could be a guest on other people's shows. My publicist, Rachel over at Sunday Brunch agency, introduced me to David. He was happy to have me on his show.

What I didn't realize was that the Monday morning that I was on his show was a Super Bowl episode. If you have been reading carefully, you can see how that would have been a major problem for me. I never watched any sports of any kind. I had not even the faintest idea of the players, in fact, I knew nothing about the game that had just been played.

To be on the show, I had to first say yes, which I did, but I never really knew that this episode was going to be all about the super bowl. Once I got there, I realized what the topic of the episode was going to be, and I couldn't really do much at that point in time. David had just gotten back from the game. Just like the popular quote, I had to "Fake it till you make it."

I played it off for a short while. Thankfully, Dave started talking about my off-road racing experience and some other things that were important for me. We actually had a good laugh about it. What resulted was that we developed a relationship and, eventually, he became my business coach.

After the episode with him on his show, I asked if we could grab a coffee to get to know him better because I was genuinely impressed by his personality and I knew I could learn a lot from him.

"Jim! I don't do coffee. I will do 15 minutes for you if you want to stop by my office, and we will catch up. Anything more than that would not be productive for me."

It did feel harsh at first, but when I took the 15 minutes opportunity, I was glad I took him up on his offer. He explained what he did, and told me that we could be friends or engage in a business relationship where he could be my coach and guide me through matters business-related. For me, the choice was simple.

"I would like to hire you as my business coach."

I worked with him for two years where he coached me about how to grow my business and opportunities. Needless to say, I learned a ton of things from him, such as focusing on my faith over fear. One of the things that resulted from this relationship was the confidence to start my own consulting business. After the initial podcast episode, I received numerous calls from people that I respected as CEOs and owners of companies, asking me for advice. They had heard my story.

Sure enough, I spoke to Dave and mentioned how so many people ended up calling me and asked me for my advice.

"Jim! That sounds a lot like consulting. It felt that way throughout the interview to me, and now, you're already in the game. Let's build a business plan around that."

It was after this experience that I decided to write down additional goals, including having a successful podcast and becoming a successful consultant. I visualized what that would look like, and I worked towards these goals non-stop.

Fast forward the 5 years, we find ourselves in the present. Dave is no longer someone I pay to be a business coach, and it has been that way for the last three years. He has become a friend, but more importantly, he reaches out to me to have guests on my podcast show. People that he thinks would be a good addition to my show, he sends them my way now. He trusts me with his clients and contacts. In addition to that, when he passes up a consulting client that may not fit his structure, he passes the lead off to me for a potential client relationship. The greatest part for me is the fact that I have seen that goal come full circle. From being a guest on a podcast to operating my own podcast, and from paying a coach to coach me to becoming a coach myself and getting paid.

There is no greater compliment than a teacher sending business to their students business, or clients to be on my podcast.

Once again, it was because I chose to write down my goals, stay disciplined, and put my blinders on to go after those goals. I had to say "Yes".

How to Write Goals?

People may be tempted to grab a pen and a paper and start listing down what they believe their goals are. That is one way to do it, but most of those goals would either be short-term or would not provide that sense of achievement or fulfillment. However, that is a part that can come later, as you can always re-evaluate your goals in line with your values and keep the ones that seem to check all the boxes.

It is important for you to write down your goals for which you must have the level of commitment and discipline to chase. Some people need step-by-step or benchmarks in order to achieve a goal. For me, once I write down the goal, I am all in and I will chase that goal with my blinders on.

Oftentimes, I keep my goals on an excel sheet, and quite a few times, I've forgotten to take a look at that excel sheet. Despite that, whenever I revisit this list, I would have already knocked off a few goals, and it would fill me with more joy to check off a goal knowing that it is achieved.

Your goals must be specific and relevant to you. Additionally, they must have a timeline, or a deadline, that you must bear in mind. There is no point in writing down a goal that reads "I want to be rich." There is no time limit to this goal, and even an additional dollar in your pocket would mean you are richer than you were a moment ago. You need to be more specific and time-bound. It is a strategy that is often used in business to plan goals. It is called SMART goals, and it means:

- Specific
- Measurable
- Attainable
- Relevant
- Time-bound

Through this strategy, you not only get to write down great goals, but you also get a clearer picture of what exactly it is that you wish to achieve. Using that, you can then use another great tool to help you achieve these goals, and that is visualization, which we discussed earlier.

Your values will transition, but for the most part, they will stay true to who you are as a human being. For me, having God as my number 1 value will never change. However, your goals can change completely. Sometimes, goals can also become irrelevant. You can always revisit them, update them, or change them altogether, as long as you keep your values in mind and plan accordingly.

I have a daily routine where I check off all the items that I have achieved during the day from my yellow pad. Next, I tear off the top of the page, rewrite my values on the top once again, just to reinforce what my values are. Then, I would review the items that I didn't complete and add in the new ones that I need to complete the next day. This is something I do every day. By doing this, I know what the next day would look like for me, and what I am expected to do throughout the day.

Quite a few times, you need to develop the momentum in the morning for the tasks and the goals for that day. The good thing is that you would have already done your homework the night before; the list that you prepared for the morning, shows you what you must do. It makes things a lot easier to achieve.

There are some instances where you may feel stuck in the day, and that is where this list can help you get back on track and pursue what you had to. How do you do that? You start to create momentum by doing the easier tasks first and cross them off, ultimately, making your way to the hard ones. Alternatively, you can do the hard ones first and the rest would look like a piece of cake to you, making the transition in the day a lot easier.

I have a lot of respect for Andy Frisella. He creates this critical task list in which he writes down five items that he has to achieve every single day, no more, no less. The idea is that once you are done with these five items, you can use the rest of your day to do anything else. However, those five items continue to evolve, grow, or evolve into something bigger and different. Over a period of time, you end up creating success, achievement of goals, and you get to experience progress in your business. But you must complete the 5 tasks no matter what.

One of the things I love telling my clients on a regular basis is to spend 5 minutes a day on the business that they wish to get themselves into and start. People often tell me how they have to work a day job, just to ensure they pay the bills, and that would often mean that they do not have much time to dedicate to this business idea. I tell them to find 5 minutes every single day and give those 5 minutes to that business. In a year from now, when people eventually do have enough time, they would have already invested significant time that they would have a collection of work that would have already been done. This provides them with a competitive advantage and a significant lead as well. If you do the numbers, you end up spending 1,825 minutes, or north of 30 hours, and that is an achievement.

You are on your way to having a business started. What matters here is consistency. Remember, it is consistency and perseverance that bring results, not speed.

It is just like trying to go to the gym. You can put in 10 hours of work in a day, but that would not be equal to the 30 minutes you spend consistently every day. It takes time and consistency to develop and manifest results. Similarly, in business, you need to be consistent.

Starting with 5 minutes or more a day you will get you there, but you need to have the discipline to go through the journey; JUST START NOW!

When I started my tequila company it came from a solid business plan. I was working a full-time, 70 plus hour a week job at Ketel One Vodka. Almost every night when I got home, after dinner, I would spend at least an hour writing my business plan. It took six months to get that plan to a place where I felt it was good enough. And even than I felt it needed to be better. I hired a professional to review the plan and enhance anything that fell short of perfect. After a $5000 fee I had perfection. Due to my time, energy, and investment; I was able to raise a 5-million-dollar commitment in investment funds for my new company. My vision to build a company with a small investment each day became a reality.

Clarity is the Key

"Get your house in order."

Sean Whalen

If you have your goals written down, and they are crystal clear, things will start working for you. Those goals will start manifesting clues and hints that something bigger is at play here. To give you an idea of how that works, let's imagine you write down a goal for yourself to a buy brand-new car by the end of this year.

That car may have already existed or might have already been out there on the streets, but you might have never noticed it. Now, when you have that goal written down and are revisiting that goal every day, you will start noticing this vehicle almost every time you drive to work, to the grocery store, or any other place. It is like your subconsciousness starts picking up the signals, making you notice things you might not have noticed otherwise. This is how the goal comes to life.

Chapter 8

Say It Out Loud

This may sound somewhat questionable to many, but as it so happens, it really isn't. Some of the easiest things to remember are the ones that you say out loud, not what you think, and speak to yourself internally.

Throughout my life, I have spoken each of the goals I wrote down out loud. I was deliberate enough to ensure that I get to hear the goals being said audible in my own voice. By doing so, not only is it me who hears this, but there is a good chance others get to hear it as well, and that's okay.

When I was young, if I would say my goals out loud, I would know that I'd be held accountable for them. Every time I would have a goal, whether related to sports or academics, I knew my parents, or my siblings would inquire about it, ask for the progress, and would probably be expecting to see some kind of result. It was this accountability that made sure I always delivered on my goals, and if I didn't, I must have a damn good reason.

When I was 21 years old, I remember vividly saying my goal out loud:

"I'm going to buy a BMW sportscar."
"Yeah, right! Whatever!"

That might not have been the kind of response I would have hoped for, but it never really mattered to me. I set a goal, said it out loud enough, and now, I had no reason not to accomplish that goal. Just two months in, I bought one for myself. Of course, that's a materialistic item, meaning that it was probably short-lived, but the principle remains. That was arguably the first goal that I said audibly enough so that other people could hear it. By doing so, I was accountable for that goal.

It is extremely critical when it comes to your health and wellness. If you can be audible about your goals, specifically your health, you will achieve that. You will also find like-minded people. If that's not enough, you'll start to eat properly. Every now and then, you'd be shown an article or two about health and fitness. The universe, will be at play, doing its thing, ensuring that all of this comes to you so that you can achieve your goals.

When you say something out loud, it becomes much easier to achieve what you believe in.

I am a big proponent of speaking something into existence. There is no denying its importance and how it tends to work. However, I believe equally as much in the concept of what you put out to the universe, the universe will deliver it back to you.

We live in a place that is ruled by an Ever-Loving God who always wants us to be happy. We have completely untapped our full potential, both physically and mentally. I think back to some of the things in my past, things that I never thought I'd be able to do on my own.

Not too long ago, I ran a 24-hour Spartan Obstacle Course race in Iceland. To make things a bit more challenging, I ran that race on a 2 weeks' notice. Earlier that year I had been training for an ultra-marathon, as a part of my spartan competitive series. I only planned on running one Ultra race in my life and that was only because a fellow competitor convinced me that the finisher "belt buckle" was worth the pain. Thanks Archie – he made me say the goal outloud! The race I chose was going to be the Lake Tahoe Spartan National Championships. Ultra-races are defined by the distance of 30 miles or more. The training itself required me to run at least 70 miles per week plus a regular weightlifting program. This was almost a full-time job.

I didn't know what to expect in Tahoe as this was my first Ultra race. What I did know is that I could rely on my training and the race strategy my coach had put together for me. The miles were long, the hills were tall, and the obstacles took every ounce of energy I had in the tank. I even encountered a bear on the course during the race. At the end of the day my training had paid off as I sprinted the last mile towards the finish line. My wife was there waiting for me as she had been my race assistant all day keeping me fueled up on Top Ramen and Coke at the halfway mark. By the way, she had already run her own 13-mile race and took the top spot on the podium. I was fortunate enough to pull off a second-place finish in my Ultra race thinking this would be my one and only at that distance.

Just two weeks after the Tahoe event, I entered a pick-up race in Arizona, which I ended up winning. This time, it was a 6-mile race, which was comparatively easier. At the finish line, I was approached by Archie again, who had put together a team to race the Spartan Ultra World championships in Iceland, which happened to be a 24-hour race. He had lost one of his team members last-minute and knew that I was "trained-up" for the long distance due to my recent race in Tahoe. He invited me to be a part of the team and even threw in taking care of the costs. It was hard to say no.

The race was just three weeks away! I mapped out my flights and training schedule against my trainer's better judgement and advice. The way I looked at it, this was a once in a lifetime opportunity. Due to flight delays and transfers, I landed in Iceland on the morning of the race that was scheduled to start at noon. I literally drove from the airport in snowy conditions to meet my team 45 minutes north of the airport in the middle of nowhere. I was completely disorientated and rushed to in a foreign country. I arrived with enough time to meet my team members for the first time and get checked in. It was a massive effort, just to find out that the "team" portion of the race was cancelled. We would be racing as individuals now. WOW! That turned fast. It was so cold at the starting line that my throat muscles were literally constricting making it hard to breath. There must have been 200 runners from around the world speaking different languages huddled together trying to stay warm anticipating the starting gun. Finally, we were off and running on one of the greatest experiences of my life. These are the times when I must remember that setting a goal and saying it outload really does work and we can all live beyond our wildest dreams. As I ascended the ice-covered slope of the first hill climb my competitive instincts kicked in. I had been running at a much slower pace than my norm, to hang with my would have been new teammates. I said my goodbyes and ratcheted up my pacc to koop up with the front runners

24-hours later, spread over 43 miles that were tracked on my Garmin, comprising of over 180 obstacles I finished the race. For men over 50, I ended up securing third place in the world. I don't know how it happened, but in the end, it happened for me, and I am glad that it did. It proves that we can do anything that we put our minds to and say the goal out loud.

It's a Daily Thing

"High achievers are at the top of their game because of the discipline they have in the unseen hours."

Alan Stein Jr.

People believe that if they say their goals out loud, or share it with someone once, it is enough. It doesn't work that way. It is, literally, a daily thing. This falls in line with being careful of what your self-talk is comprised of because if you write down a goal, speak it out loud every day, and then feed yourself with negativity, it is not going to work.

Our subconscious mind is powerful, but not many people know that. It is designed to take everything as a fact, meaning that it cannot distinguish between what can be and what can't be. It cannot differentiate between what's real and what isn't. This is why whatever we tell ourselves, our subconscious mind accepts it as the truth and starts working around it. If we were to say, "I can't do that," our subconscious mind will overlook whether we have the capability to do something, and instead focus on channeling all your energy into other places so that you either avoid what you believe you can't do or ensure your own failure if you still pursue it.

This is also true because if we meditate and visualize, our subconscious mind starts accepting that as the truth as well. This is why I mentioned just how important and powerful it is to visualize your goals. The more you do it, the more your subconscious mind will work towards finding ways to make it a reality.

Think about it. Take any of your recent drives from point A to point B, let's say from work to home, can you recall 100% of your trip from your workplace to your home? Can you recall how many red lights you encountered, or how many vehicles you passed, or just how many signs you came across, saw, and followed? Most likely, you can't recall most of those details, and that is because your conscious mind was preoccupied thinking about something else entirely. If that is the case, which it is, then who was driving? That was your subconscious mind doing it. Why? Because you believed you would reach home on time, safely, and easily. Your subconscious mind complied, and it did exactly that.

You are a product of what you believe in and what you think. We are constantly putting thousands of thoughts into our minds every day. With so many thoughts, it is easy to start your day with the wrong thought. Once again, if you practice gratitude, and you begin your first thought of the day on a positive note, you will start and finish your day on a high note. The opposite is also true because if you wake up thinking "God! I don't want to go to work today," you are going to have a long, tiring, and cumbersome day. Whatever you start your day with, you become that person for the rest of the day.

The biggest challenge you have every single morning is to control your thoughts and ensure you start on the right foot.

"Discipline equals freedom. There is no shortcut, there is no hack, there's only one way so get after it."

Jocko Willink

Part of my training regime for spartan racing is to run my property. My property is a solid half-a-mile loop with some up and down hills. When I am training for long distances, I often end up doing 8 to 12 miles in my yard, in the snow, with temperatures often dropping below zero. My first thought is always to visualize the finish line of the spartan race, wherever it may be held, and me crossing it as the winner. I visualize the entire race while I am running around my yard, thinking about the finish lines, the competitors, the obstacles, and so on. Every training mile becomes a race for me in my mind.

Visualization on Steroids

I have a goal on my list to buy a 20-acre property next to my house. So, as I am visualizing the spartan race while running around my yard, I come across a fence that overlooks that property. I look over at the fence line and tell myself, "I'm going to own you one day. That's my property." I take my time to admire the view and visualize where I would park my car, how I would use the land to graze cattle and extend my current ranch. As soon as I turn away from that property, I am back visualizing the race itself. That is literally visualization and positive talks on steroids.

For two and a half years, I have lived on this property and spoken about owning the 20 acres one day. The owner, as it turns out, did not want to sell it initially. He finally caved in and decided to sell the property. He didn't take the price I had offered him and ended up selling it to a third party. However, despite that, I have now leased 10-acres of that property from the new owner where I am able to raise my cattle on and achieve the goal I had envisioned. It was simply because I manifested that reality in my mind. I achieved a portion of that goal, and that is just another step that brings me closer to my ultimate goal.

"As you think, so shall you become!"

Bruce Lee

People underestimate what they can achieve in life if they put their minds to something. They limit themselves, through their own limiting beliefs that are either imposed upon them from childhood or are dictated by society. I have talked to Dave about donating 8% of our gross profit to the orphanages in Mexico. The first thing he said:

"Why would you limit yourself? Why just limit yourself to 8%? Why not say that you are going to be the largest contributor to orphanages in Baja?"

I immediately knew he had a point. While I jumped to the "limited," he jumped to the "limitless." It shows that we truly do not understand what we are capable of doing.

Chapter 9

Live With Your Decisions

Whether you make the right decision or wrong, learn how to live with it. This is far more important of a lesson, and yet, most of us have no idea how this helps us become better decision-makers and better people.

Earlier in the book I referenced that Surfers make better CEO's. There is an opportunity to look at many parts of our life to understand that we have the capability to make decisions and stick with them. Sometimes those decisions might not be popular amongst your circle of friends, but they could be the right ones for you. It's unfortunate that we allow our influencers to change our minds about the decisions that we make. If we understand our true values and goals, then the decisions we make should be aligned with who we are. Don't let anyone or anything change that.

If a CEO can spot a wave of opportunity, they can decide almost instantly whether they want to be a part of that wave and ride it all the way in or see if they crash and burn. A true CEO will take full responsibility for their decision and will stick to it regardless of the outcome.

This is also why I believe that extreme sports athletes also make great CEOs. When you look at the boardroom, the board table, people that are trying to make a decision are usually busy going through every possible outcome. Ask yourself, what's the worst that can happen? You might run into something that isn't favorable, have another meeting, and redirect your goals or objectives. That's it. The wrong decision may cost you money or setbacks, but at least your life won't be on the line like these extreme athletes.

I can make the wrong decisions because I know that I can always correct the errors or learn something from them to ensure they don't happen again. At the same time, I know this wrong decision, if it turns out to be one, will not mean an end to my life. On the other hand, the very same decision can turn out to be the best decision of my life, and it would feel great knowing that I decided in a split second, without wasting time on deliberations.

Finishing The Race

In my racing career, I was fortunate. I have raced in more events than the average team owner in a top-level professional class. If that wasn't enough, I also owned a vintage race car, famous in the 70s. It was the infamous 1957 Chevy that was built to go off-road. In its day, that car won 48 races, 3 Baja 1000 championships, and many others. I was fortunate enough to acquire the vehicle from the original owner, Larry Schwocoffer. I bought the race car to enter it into the NORRA Vintage 1000, a recreation of the original Baja 1000 races. When this car entered, it was instantly one of the main attractions. The off-road community knew the history of this vehicle and appreciated the vintage orange color we had painted it. The Baja locals also loved the car, I think that had to do with the loud pipes and the fact we were a front runner on the course. In fact, whenever I stopped, people would come out of their homes, asking me to sign an autograph for them on Hot Wheels that looked like the iconic 57 Chevy.

In one particular year, Marty Fiolka, who was responsible for most of the PR at the events, approached me and said:

"Jim! You're racing in this race. I would love to put the editor-in-chief of Hot Rod Magazine in your car and integrate her with your race team. Would you mind?"

It took a couple of months to formulate a plan for this to work, but I would never pass up this opportunity. Elana was the editor-in-chief for the famous Hot Rod Magazine, and she was a huge car fanatic. I met her the night before the race. The idea was to follow the car 1,000 miles throughout the region for the next five days. We had, on a whim, decided that on day 3 she would get in the race car with me and help me reach one of the main pitstops a couple hundred miles south.

In the morning, we got her suited up in a race outfit, helmet, walked her through the responsibilities and the car itself. We have been doing this for a long time, but the reality would always be the same for everyone, regardless of their experience. If they can hang on long enough and warn the driver of any impending threat or danger, it should work out just fine. A driver can only concentrate and anticipate what's about to come, but the assistant is the one who warns the person with pace notes on what's about to come so that the driver knows full well and prepares accordingly. The hardest part is knowing there left from the right hand, just ask Darryl!

We hit the starting line, took off, and everything was going great. We were in the front of the class for the first two days. The car was running impeccably. Often the course can be treacherous, and you will take some hits and dings. We also got tangled up with a Jeep 4x4, but we managed to continue going strong. About halfway through the day, the oil temperature and pressure started rising. We were losing oil fast. The crew had suggested that we had to stop. We had a bad oil leak coming out of the front seal. We carry spare oil on a rack in the cab of the car, so I poured everything we had into the motor. After careful evaluation, Elana suggested we had a blown motor, and we would have to quit!

About this time, a Canadian husband and wife on vacation stopped by to say hello in their Subaru wagon. They asked if we needed help or a tow. I laughed them off and said we were just fine. There was no way in hell I was going to let a Canadian couple in a Subaru tow me out of the toughest racecourse in North America. They decided to park alongside the course to take pictures and watch us figure out our problems.

Me being the man that I am, and the mechanically inept that I am, I neglected the idea of quitting the race now. Despite my best efforts, we were dead in the water. I had to tuck my tail between my legs and go ask for the Canadians to save the day. The Subaru was going to pull us out of the desert the next 15 miles to the main highway where the team awaits me. I had the pleasure of staring at the tow line in front of me for 2 hours as the vacationers took pictures and drank some cold ones all the way to civilization. While being towed, Elana asked what we going to do next. Well, I wasn't going to quit that easy, that's for sure. When we got to the highway, we were greeted with an astounding number of children and race fans, looking for autographs. I went to the team captain and asked where we were. I was told that they we were near Loreto, and he had arranged to buy a motor from a local mechanic when we got there. We could work over night and put the new motor in the car. Since this was a 5-day race, you could have a DNF or time out for a day and continue to race the next day.

The motor was a no-show, but the next morning one of the security personnel explained how his father-in-law had a 1987 chevy pick-up that we could buy and use the motor from. This is how Mexico works, there is always a solution and someone willing to help. We connected with the truck owner at his buddy's shop that we rented for the day. The cost was $50 dollars and some cerveza to do the work there. The incredible thing was that half the men in this small town showed up to watch us do the motor swap and video live feeds back to Hot Rod magazine in the USA. Halfway through the day a local fisherman showed up with two, five-gallon buckets filled with fresh clams and tortillas. They made a feast to go with the beer and tacos we had bought for everyone. *Pause here – these are memories that last a lifetime*. We rallied the team and eight hours later, the motor was swapped, and we were ready to get back in the race. Eventually, we were able to finish the iconic Baja 1000 in a 1957 Chevy, something many thought would no longer be possible.

With a podium finish, we ended up getting 7 pages written about us in the Hot Rod Magazine. This was all because of the “Never quit” attitude and willingness to figure out a solution that ensured our victory. And by the way, the magazine coverage helped secure several new sponsors for the following year.

Stop Worrying About What Can Happen

People who think too much about what might happen or think of how things can go wrong, know that the waves may come and go, but a good wave is rare to get. If you miss the opportunity, someone else will take it, and ride the wave, leaving you regretting not making the decision sooner. This also goes for business as there are many great opportunities that surround us every day. People just get too intimidated about taking these opportunities that someone else usually ends up taking full advantage explore them.

The reason this happens is that we tend to focus far too much on the “can’t” part and forget to shine some light on the “can” part.

It’s time that we get off our **“BUT’s”** – Get after it!

Instead of worrying about if’s and buts, let’s make a change and grab the opportunity while it’s still there. Take it from me, there is a 9 out of 10 chance that you will encounter a reward at the other end of the opportunity. Rarely do you come across something that doesn't work for you or causes you a marginal loss. It is better to try and learn than to pass on it and regret it later.

It is cliché to say that my glass is half-full, but it is never half-full for me. I am always looking for the opportunity. When everyone is busy saying "We can't," I am out there trying to figure out a reason why I should. I know that this is where I will find my competitive advantage, as you will see in the next chapter.

Chapter 10

The Holiday Advantage

I love long weekends, not because I get to stay home and do nothing. Instead, I love the fact that everyone's not working on Mondays or other scheduled days off, chilling, relaxing, perhaps even traveling, and while they do that, I am up and running, working throughout the days. Why? Because I love the fact that I am getting ahead of so many people. While they continue to do things that may be unproductive in nature, I am doing what I do best, and generating more revenue for myself and my business.

With this mindset, I always get to have a competitive edge over my competitors because they chose to prioritize taking special days off. Make no mistake here, I am not trying to instill the idea that holidays are bad because they aren't. Everyone needs them, and that includes me as well. However, the point I am trying to make is that I am more interested in seeking out the competitive advantage, and it is often found when others are resting. I like to pick my own days off verse the "Hallmark Holidays" we are forced to take.

The last two years of mine have been a wonderful experience in my business, despite the so-called pandemic that has affected our lives. I have looked at that as an opportunity to work from home, explore all the possible areas that I find interesting, and make more money than ever before by helping others make more money as well. It is always about how do we leverage the tools that we have in front of us or improve upon what we have been doing while everyone has been asleep at the wheel. Then, there is the fact that most of these competitors are affected by the negativity, whether because of the pandemic or something within the society and even there you can find an opportunity to get ahead of your competitors. You will always be able to find something to become better at, to do better, and to prove that you are better if you seek out the opportunities.

Being Ahead of the Pack

One of my favorite times of year happens to be Christmas time. I am with my kids, just like everyone else, but unlike others, I do not take two weeks off and forget about my work completely. I have been working for the last 30 years, and that's enough experience for me to learn that most businesses tend to shut down between December 15th to the start of the new year. For me, that's a great time to work on my plans, strategy, and get ahead of the rest of the competition. Through my plans, I am always ready to make sure that I attack their businesses on day one or go after the business myself and do hand-selling, just to accommodate for any shortcomings.

I am programmed to seek out those little windows of opportunities that most tend to overlook. While others may prioritize comfort, I prioritize seeking out opportunities. My goal and I am not shy to share this, is to stay several steps ahead of my competitors. Through that window of opportunity, I always end up creating a gap between me and my competitors to try and fulfill. While they are catching up, I am seeking the next best way to increase that gap and extend my lead even further.

This is coming from my competitive sports side that I brought into my business, but it is something that helps me stretch that lead significantly. This also means that while others may be catching up, I get the chance to slow down, take a breather, reanalyze my strategies, move forward and still be in the lead. At no point during this time am I worried about others catching up to me. The same happens when I am also with my customers as I get ahead of them and before they even think about it, I know what they want and need.

Most people are always looking for a reason to take a break, just because everyone is doing the same thing. To me, taking a day off for no reason makes no sense at all. Since people look for breaks, I correlate that to them understanding what their true values and goals are. They are walking through life every day, without realizing the cause and effect that it will bring. If my daughter comes up to me and asks if I could spend the day with her, I can say “yes” because I know I am operating in the positive margin. I can afford the time away because its “in the bank”.

Just this past summer, my daughter came up to me and said:

“Hey, Dad! Wouldn’t it be great to take a month off this year?” I looked at her for a minute before coming up with an answer. “You know what? You’re right. I’m going to take a month off.”

I ended up taking the entire month of July off minus a couple phone calls. This was only because I was ahead of my game plan, and I had prepared for being flexible when I wanted to be. When I did go back to the work after 30 days, I was where I knew I would be because everything was already aligned.

There are those who may view the entire concept of working on holidays or starting the day at 5 AM instead of 9

AM as a way to steal time away from their families, and that's their opinion. For me, I look at that as opening up a gap of opportunity for me to have more time to spend with my family, without worrying about the effects it would have on me or my business.

Not Just Holidays

You can actually find these windows of opportunity almost every single day. This is exactly what some of the most successful people on earth do, and this is why they start their day at 5 AM instead of 9 AM. While the world starts at the usual 9'o clock, the early morning starters already gather an unassailable 4 hours of lead. Regardless of what the competitors do, they cannot even come close to the lead that these people have amassed.

We all have access to one of the greatest tools ever invented, a cell phone. If I can structure my days, take advantage of opportunities to conduct businesses to free up time later in the day, I am better for it, more efficient for it, and my customers are happier for it. I always seek out whatever tools I have in my reach, ensure that I utilize them fully, and draw out the results that I need. It could be a resource book from one of my shelves that I may be able to correlate to a written response on an email, or if it's my computer to use and search through Google, create spreadsheets, I use them all.

David Meltzer gave me quite a lot of tips, and one, for which I am thankful, is to view your calendar and search out the white spaces. He explained how that whitespace is an opportunity that is staring at you. Confused? Let me explain.

If you use a calendar, whether hand-written or digital, and you schedule all your work accordingly, and you still end up with big whitespaces. Think about how you can best utilize those spaces. This would not only be for your personal values or goals, but it could also be to spend time with your family, learning something new, working on your health and fitness, taking up a new challenge or hobby, et cetera. Once you start becoming efficient in utilizing the whitespace in your calendar, not only will you see yourself spending more time with your family, but you will also be able to realize massive gains in your business.

People struggle to understand what they are capable of doing. This happens because they haven't dug deep enough to figure that part out, and because of that, they are bounding around in life, with literally no direction. I recently bumped into this wonderful woman and she happens to have an incredible resume. She wanted to undergo a career change. As usual I went through her resume, asked her what kind of business she intended to pursue, and so on. The trouble was that we live in a small town, and given her banking experience, it would only fetch her a limited result.

"Have you ever thought about business consulting?"
"No! I haven't. Why would you suggest that?"
"You have a vast background of experience that people would love to have. Understanding what your values and goals are, fits in line. You might find a lot more success through this than going to work for another employer."

What she failed to realize was her own strength. It was right there, right in front of her. It was her experience and the knowledge that she had amassed through that experience.

People only deal with their shortcomings and don't really focus on the bigger picture. Once you are able to get past that, it is then a matter of utilizing time to your advantage and understanding that it is your friend. You can then use the time to structure a lot of things in life, business, and more.

My Strengths?

"The vision that you glorify in your mind, the ideal that you enthrone in your heart- this you will build your life by, this you will become."

James Allen

I am what you would call a strategist. If I was coaching someone on personal matters, and they had a wonderful business but were suffering due to their personal matters, I would still try and find the goodness they may be overlooking. In one case, I held a few meetings with a client and quickly realized that this person had a business opportunity that they weren't taking advantage of. Seeing the opportunity, I offered my services and extended them from personal coaching to business coaching. I was even offered an opportunity to partner up in that business. While they may not have seen something, I saw the opportunity. I could have easily seized the moment for this person, but I wanted the client to see it first.

My career background is colorful, and that is probably an understatement. I am often asked if there is anything that I haven't done in life. That is because I have been involved in many, many areas. From the race trucks to business coaching, and everything in between. You name it, I have done it. Because I always had the willingness to try it first and see what comes out of the opportunity. During my entire life, I have had a lot of fun and a lot of success that I have gathered throughout my years.

I would certainly encourage you to do the same and discover more in life because it is the willingness to take the opportunity first and worrying about the results later that may help you figure out what you really love and enjoy.

The advantage comes down to authenticity. By being yourself and who you are, whether in business or personal life, you allow people to see who you really are and what you truly stand for. If you love your country, and you love God, and people get to see that, you already get to start your relationship on a far stronger foundation as opposed to not showing who you truly are and leaving them to assume who you may or may not be.

When someone understands that you have faith in life, they will automatically be inclined to believe that you wouldn't cheat or lie your way through with your partner or clients. By knowing the true authentic self and conveying that message to your clients, you will have an authentic competitive edge to win with.

Chapter 11

Make the Deal at the Top

"Skill can be developed over time, but your attitude can be adjusted in a single moment of clarity."

Leslie Zann

One of the most common things that you will find is just how easily people are intimidated by the ones who sit at the top of the food chain or hierarchy. It could be in the world of sports, stardom, business, and even in general life. People are simply afraid to approach the person at the top.

I was fortunate enough during my tenure with Ketel One vodka that I oversaw the sponsorships for the company.

One of my greatest accomplishments was that I worked with the late great Arnold Palmer and Peter Jacobson. We spent over a year trying to integrate Ketel One Vodka as the official alcohol sponsor of the PGA Tour. To some, this might come as a surprise, but as it turns out, the PGA Tour is quite a conservative setup, meaning that they never truly had any official distilled spirit as a sponsor. It took one year of hard work and planning, but eventually, it was decided that Ketel One would become the official sponsor. Although, we had to come up with a very creative direction that didn't take away anything from the values of the organization and what they wanted to promote to their customers.

Between myself, Arnold Palmer, Peter Jacobson, and the executives of the company, we came up with a traveling Arnold Palmer Museum at the major PGA touring events. The idea was to set up a museum, based on side-by-side trailers, where people could view 100 artifacts from Arnold Palmer's life on display. While they were there, they were able to sample a Ketel One martini. That is what allowed us to have branding on site. I was fortunate enough to go to Arnold's home and pick out those 100 items with my business colleague Amy. We were like two kids in a historic candy store of golf history.

To see a person of his caliber, and what he had accomplished in his illustrious career, was no less of a privilege. One of my favorite artifacts in the completed museum was his very first expense tracking report that his wife had maintained for him. When you looked at it, you realized that he only made $120 at the golf tournament, $15 of which went towards travel, $5 towards food, and it just felt unreal.

What I learned is that it is perfectly okay to work at the top. Do not be intimidated by anyone's stature, even that of Arnold Palmer or Peter Jacobson. There is no point in thinking that you can't do anything with them just because you perceive them to be out of reach. They aren't. They are normal human beings, just like you and me. They too want to conduct business just as much as you do. They too want to accomplish many great things just as you do. If you have the confidence to reach out, you will find success.

I learned this lesson and have always ensured that I apply what I learned. Now, I look for possible opportunities, and if I see one, I am no longer afraid to reach out to the people at the very top of the game. And who knows, they might just make you laugh.

One morning I was in the hotel lobby before a big golf tournament waiting for my staff. Arnold Palmer approached me from across the room with a grin on his face almost laughing at something. He said "Jim, every night before I go to bed my wife sets out a glass of water and my pills for the next morning. That way I don't forget to take them. Well, this morning I grabbed those pills and chugged down the water so fast, I didn't realize I had grabbed the half full, left-over glass of Ketel One vodka from the night before. I guess it's going to be one hell of a day for golf" as he walked away laughing.

The Ice Display

Part of our work at Ketel One involved donating ice displays to the PGA tour, to pour martinis through them, at most of the opening events. I was in Rhode Island for the opening night of their big tournament. I could pick out all the greatest golfers in the sport walking around the event. I did not expect Greg Norman (The Shark) to walk over and shake my hand while introducing himself. He wanted to tell me how much he enjoyed the ice display we had brought to the party. I am guessing not as much as I envied his 70 million dollar mega yacht. Either way, he wanted to know why he didn't have this fantastic ice display at his event in Florida.

"Well Greg, I love your tournament. We do have a lot of fans down there in Florida. As a matter of fact, Peter Jacobson lives near your tournament venues, in Naples, Florida. However, your tournament director doesn't feel like we are a good fit, and I think it's worth talking about."

Trust me, it takes a whole lot of confidence to say this to the man, the shark himself, Greg Norman. Just because we were in a social gathering, he said:

"Look! I don't have time to discuss this right now, but why don't you meet me tomorrow at the golf course? You can walk some holes with me, have a late lunch, and I do understand that you are going to Chicago tomorrow. As it turns out, so am I. How about you fly there with me and we can talk about this?"

There's one rule that happens to be absolute and unchanged, and that is "You cannot say no to the shark." I knew he purchased a luxurious private jet, so I knew I wasn't going to pass on this opportunity.

The next morning, I headed to the golf course, met Greg and his people. As planned, I walked with him through a couple of holes. We discussed golf, laughed, and joked, and had a great lunch together in the clubhouse. Soon, we got on one of the four transportation vehicles on our way to the airport. When we got there, I saw dozens of pro-golfers. With them, myself, and Greg walking, I was wondering just how big his jet was going to be in order to accommodate all of us. Moments later, the entire group turned left, and Greg and I went right along with his personal assistants. Just four of us were going to his jet while others would have to make do in something else. I later learned that the jet was only on its second flight since it had been built. It was a brand-new Gulfstream 550 that holds up to 19 passengers – this was top of the line.

The jet took off, and we enjoyed some ice-cold drinks during the flight. During that time, we worked out a plan and negotiated a deal to work on his tournament. Our participation included a free trip to an extravagant golf outing that would take place at the end of the year. Greg's tournament director did not want the winners to wait a full year to go on that trip. Greg, however, thought:

"It's such a special trip. People would probably wait a year or more just to get a chance to take part. There shouldn't be any reason why you shouldn't be included in this event."

As fate would have it, we signed a deal on that flight, from Rhode Island to Chicago, to be involved at Greg's event. Even though I am no longer with Ketel One, as far as I know, they are still participating in those events.

All of this can be boiled down to the fact that I found the confidence within me to speak and interact directly with the man on the very top. I said yes to the shark, I spoke my mind with him, and I negotiated a deal after changing all my plans to suit his, and I wasn't afraid at all. I still feel bad that my business colleague Amy had to fly commercial that day.

They're Just Like Us

While you can continue to look at the people on the very top and find yourself intimidated, take a step back, relax, and understand that they are just like you and me. They are people with pretty much the same needs as anyone else. They too want to negotiate good business deals, accomplish their goals, find success, get to know good and interesting people, and even enjoy life where they can. There is no reason to be intimidated by the stature or the job title that they may carry. That is more of a psychological barrier that most of us try not to breach. However, if you find that confidence within you to reach out to them, speak to them, and propose a good business, they may never turn you down.

Those who find themselves being intimidated are only limited by their own beliefs and fears. This bars them from becoming the people at the top, and while they do that, someone else might just walk through those doors, approach the same people, and work their way into a deal that could have been yours for the taking.

I have had the pleasure, to meet some of the top celebrities in entertainment and sports in my life. Only a few, out of numerous, weren't the kindest, nicest, most grateful people on the planet. Once you allow yourself to understand that these people are pretty much like anyone else around us, you then enable yourself to have the confidence to speak to the real decision-makers and find success of a completely new height and magnitude.

These interactions, on a more casual basis with the people at the top, had built my confidence to have interactions when they really meant the most to me. When I was starting my tequila company, I knew I needed to raise around $5 million in order to garner the kind of results I wanted. Through my years of working with Peter Jacobson, he had always treated me with respect and told me what a great job I was doing. He was the one who said if I was going to do anything besides Ketel One, I should let him know. I am the kind of guy who believes that when people say that, most of the time they mean that. However, one of the harder calls that I had to make, was to call and ask him if he would invest in my new business. Around this time, I was second-guessing my confidence. As I was dialing the number, I stopped for a second before hitting the dial button and thought to myself if I should really be calling him to ask for money. The answer should always be "Yes" without question, particularly in my case as he had respected me, given me accolades, and praised my method of work, and even offered to partner up in future ventures that I may have besides Ketel One.

There are times where I hesitate, despite having all the confidence in the world, but if that ever happens, I remind myself just how important it is for me to follow my gut and look at the facts that were right there before me. It doesn't take more than a split second for me to regain my composure, confidence, and hit the dial button to make that all-important call of the day. I did make the call that day. He invited me to Naples, Florida, and said he wanted to invest in the company and wanted me to meet other people who were also likely to invest in my company.

We were going raise $3 million to start, and we ended up raising $12 million over a period of years instead.

Never back out of an opportunity to speak with the people at the very top. There are hundreds of deals you can make with the people at your level or those under you, but you will always be bombarded with limiting beliefs, questions that have obvious answers, and yet people overlook those. Instead, focus on the people at the very top. They are the people who truly understand what they are getting into and will provide you with not just the finances or the assistance you need to get started, but they can often open doors towards other opportunities that would further compliment your efforts and your confidence to reach out to them.

Chapter 12

Asking for Help

Are you someone who is ashamed of asking others for help? If you are, you are just like most of us. I don't know when we started being embarrassed or afraid to ask for help as a society, but it's time to change the narrative.

Let's make one thing clear. You cannot achieve the type of success any of us would want, without having help. If you want to buy a house, you go to the bank to assist you in the purchase. If you want to invest in some business opportunity, you ask for answers and advice from those who may be able to help you out. If you feel depressed, anxious, and worried, you seek medical assistance. We all need help in almost every aspect of our lives. Since that is the case, at what point did asking for help in business become a thing to be embarrassed about?

It's Okay to Ask

One of the hardest things for us to do, especially as successful entrepreneurs and adults, is to seek help. For some reason, we have this immensely negative belief that asking for help translates to "We don't know." If we can get past our egos and realize that no one on earth knows everything, asking for help becomes a lot easier.

It is one of the most important tools that we have in our arsenal that literally costs us nothing but yields a result that not many other tools can bring to you. What's more interesting is the fact that we are always quick to offer help to others, and we do it almost immediately. When you meet a new neighbor, and you want to make a good impression on them, you typically offer help to ensure that they know you are a good person. It is human nature to offer help in one way or another.

This is true in literally every case and scenario of our lives. If someone is sick, we offer them help. If someone joins a new job, others rush in to offer help. If someone needs to cross the road, we would offer help. If we are so eager to offer help, why are we so against the idea of seeking help ourselves? It doesn't make any sense. It is perfectly okay to ask for help when you feel like you need it.

As a business owner and an entrepreneur, we must know and appreciate the importance of seeking help. It is through seeking help from others that we get exposed to other opportunities. It is by asking for help from others that we get to have great partners in our businesses. It is also through asking for help that we often encounter new arenas, deals, and other lucrative opportunities that could net results that we would have never been able to acquire otherwise.

By asking for help, you are breaking down barriers that may exist in relationships. In the end, this only makes you more approachable. Why? After asking for help and showing your determination, commitment, and willingness to learn, adapt, and succeed, people will rely on you, trust you, and might even seek you out to be the person they would want to work with when opportunities come their way. It also shows we are humble and honest about our shortcomings.

Did I Ever Ask for Help?

I know! Many of you might have this question on your mind right now. It is only fair on my part to ensure I answer that question for you.

One of the things about working in the golf industry for all those years; I don't golf. To be honest, I really don't care for golf. I can barely pick up a club, and I was told at a very young age that if I wanted to succeed in business, I had to learn how to play golf. For me, that was a direct reason for never playing golf because I wanted to prove them wrong. I got to a point where I had to realize and accept that I had to learn it.

At the highpoint of my Ketel One career we were working with some top athletes. One of which was Pro golfer Scott McCarron. We had a big event in Scottsdale, Az at the Westin Kierland Hotel. I connected with Scott the afternoon before our event which overlooked the golf course. If you have ever been there, you know how great the view is looking towards the green. I mentioned to Scott that I really needed to get a golf lesson and step up my game. I had zero golf skills at the time. Scott said to me, "Jim, just ask if you want me to show you some basic golf skills so you can go out and have some fun at all these events we are doing". I immediately mustered up the courage to ask him to help me and created a window of opportunity the following morning before our guests arrived. The fact is, I had a great time with Scott, and I learned enough to make the activity more pleasurable. I still don't golf that often, but when I do, I follow the advice Scott gave me that day. Besides, not many people can say they were taught how to play by a PGA touring pro.

As an owner of two companies, and having run several others, I realized where my weaknesses are, and that is in accounting. I love to crunch the numbers and analyze them, but when it comes to putting them together, working on QuickBooks, I can't do that on my own. I had to ask for help so many times and eventually had to find the right accounting professional to do the job for me. If I had to be successful, I had to ensure that I either learn how to do that or have someone who knows it to handle the job for me. I had to surround myself with the right people, and in my world, that would be the right CPA and the right accountant. Throughout my career, I have asked people to help me with my accounts because I cannot do it. Had I been ashamed, embarrassed, or too shy to ask for help, I would have never had the kind of success that I do today.

You don't just ask for people who are above you for help. You can always ask for help from people working around you, or for you. That's the recipe of success, and yet, people tend to avoid that part completely. There is nothing wrong with doing that, and it shouldn't be a matter of ego because asking for help doesn't really make you look any smaller. If anything, there are two benefits you go on to get:

1. You get your job done properly
2. You allow someone else to feel important, especially if that person happens to be your subordinate or a member of your team that works for you.

It is a classical win-win scenario. There is absolutely no losing side here and both of you are walking away with your head held high.

Mentors are Helpers Too

We entrepreneurs and business owners know all about mentors, who they are, what they do, and just how incredibly important their contributions can be in your life, both personal and business. While many would argue that we "hire" mentors, what we are effectively doing is seeking their assistance, asking them for help. It is their experience, vast knowledge, and their superior expertise in what they do that allows them to help people from all walks of life learn to become successful.

Help isn't necessarily limited to financial assistance. Similarly, mentors are people we hire to "help" us build a better future, a better business, and carve a path for us personally and professionally.

I do the very same thing. People from all over the country come to me for help in establishing their businesses, transitioning from one industry to another, and ensuring that everything goes smoothly. They rely on my input, my expertise to ensure that they can fully discover their strengths and weaknesses and build a career based on those strengths, values, and beliefs. My job is literally to help them figure that out and layout the plan for them.

I had a great guest on my podcast named Alan Stein. He had written the critically acclaimed book titled *Raise Your Game*, and he happens to be one of the best performance coaches in basketball. What I learned from him while doing the show was that even the greatest of greats has a coach. Think about it. The top teams in the business still have a coach that teaches them and ensures that they practice their basics properly to perform the best in the upcoming tournaments. They all perform at the top of their capacity. If that is the case, why wouldn't that be equally important in business to have a coach, a mentor, to help you through all the ups and downs of the business world? It makes sense, right?

Just a 15-minute call with a mentor can keep you in line with what your goals are, and what I have learned is you often don't realize what you need until you have a coach point it out. All of a sudden, a barrage of questions pour out in those 15 minutes of coaching calls where you don't only ask for help but seek advice to improve, to become better at what you do. In the last 5 years, I have added a professional coach to my career, on a regular basis. I have been involved in a coaching session between 2 to 4 times a month, just so I could be coached. For me, that's my way of asking for help. This is what allows me to maintain my businesses, and to help them grow beyond what I believe is possible.

Ask any basketball fan who the greatest player of all time was, and everyone would name Michael Jordan, and for good reasons. However, despite him being the king of the hill, he had a coach too, and that was Tim Grover. It was his coach that ensured he knew what he had to do every single time he went out to the court and delivered his A-game.

Despite all that, there are those who would question the need of hiring a coach. These are the people who would look at the cost of hiring a coach and think "That's probably not worth the money."

Where you put your money, you put your attention, and where you put your attention, you get results!

Free information may be available all around the internet, but what good is it to you if it can't improve anything that you are doing already? I am in the habit of giving as often as I can in my life. Being a professional and personal coach and consultant, I often give my time away to clients. What I found was when I give my time away, I end up with the least results and the least amount of success. There is simply no accountability there.

When you place a value on something, you will get equal value back. When you are working with a coach, it is important that you know your values clearly as it will ensure you are more specific in your actions and gain results quicker. If for some reason, you don't know your values, you are setting yourself up for failure.

The best scenarios involve exchanging value for value. This is why we charge what we charge because if I was to give 30 minutes of my time for free, provide free advice to everyone, I would not gain anything, and on top of that, the other person would easily be bored or find everything I am saying worth ignoring. The reason that happens is that they never paid anything for the 30 minutes of information, and whatever is free is usually not that attractive. This principle fits perfectly in all areas of business and life.

If I was to sell a company, I would only be able to do that if I was providing equal value for the buyers and the sellers. Through working together, we ensure that we meet somewhere in the middle where everyone walks away happy. If it was all value for me as the seller, I might walk away wealthier and happier, but I couldn't live with the fact that the buyer never got the kind of value they were hoping for in return. This would also create tension for any referrals or potential deals down the road. This is why I firmly believe in providing equal value for value.

Chapter 13

Your Actions Speak Louder Than Words

This is arguably the most famous saying out there, and one that has a point that is proven repeatedly. I am a consultant, and it is due to the nature of my expertise and job that I observe your actions more than the words you speak. You may talk about how you want to have a healthy life, reduce your weight, regain the lost energy, and bring a dramatic change, but it wouldn't mean that you would do it. It is the actions you take, that you follow up with, that truly paint the real picture, and that is something I am more interested in. Your actions can determine the kind of person you are. I can take one quick glance through your calendar and tell you if you are going to achieve success or not. Similarly, an accountant can view your accounts and let you know if the chart is pointing the right way up. It's all about your actions.

I have an acquaintance that is a major influencer in business and social media. We have spoken live on the phone a few times and they have even been a guest on my podcast. We often like one another's post on social media which is to say we remain on each other's radar. At this point I felt comfortable enough to ask this person if they would share a quote about me for this book. It seemed like a small enough request for a busy person. The immediate response I received was "Absolutely"! It felt great that they were willing to chip in on my effort to push out this book with some endorsements. The "yes" I received was never acted upon, so I waited a couple weeks to ask again. Now the response was "what exactly do you want me to do anyway"? After clarifying again and giving a very specific example to the point where I almost wrote the entire thing, I received a heart emoji back. I presume that's still a yes, or at least it wasn't a no. As of the writing of this book and several attempts to politely let this person know about my deadlines, I'm still waiting. The point of this story is to illustrate that you can say something repeatedly in different ways, but until you generate ACTION – it doesn't matter what you say. Especially if you preach to people on how to get shit done

The Shopping Cart Incident

My wife and I were on our monthly trip to Costco to drop another paycheck on food and things we don't need. We brought our two daughters along which were 3 and 5 at the time. As we exited the store with two full baskets and our kids in tow, my wife veered right while I was going straight. She hollered at me and the kids to keep going and she was going to catch up. About that time, she arrived at a vehicle with its trunk open while the owner was sitting in a wheelchair by herself trying to load groceries. As I walked away with the kids, we all looked back to see that mom was helping this person unload the groceries from the cart into the trunk. A short while later she made it back to our car and helped us finish loading our own stuff. We didn't exchange any words until we got back in the car with the kids. I asked, "what was that all about". She said "I want our kids to see us do the things we talk about. If we are going to be a family that talks about helping others, we better show them whenever we can". Proud to be her husband, I didn't say another word all the way home.

Andy's Take

One of my current business coaches, Andy Frisella, gives a gross example on how to sum up an individual. If you read through the lines and get the real message, it is powerful.

"I can summarize everything I need to know about a person if they leave the piss on the seat of the toilet!"

What he means is that it shows just how disrespectful and irresponsible a person is by doing something like that and leaving without bothering to clean up the mess for the next person. It shows that some people do not pay heed or show any care for the other person who may have to clean up their mess, sit on it without realizing it's there, or even look at the mess. It indicates that this person may be selfish, and not the kind of a person I, or anyone else for that matter, would want to interact with.

Small actions can often provide significant clues about who you are dealing with. From the way they talk to the way they behave and act when in certain situations, you can often find out far more about the person than what they may tell you.

Back in the days when I had to conduct a lot of business meetings during lunch, I had a rule. I typically only took meetings with strangers that wanted to do business with my company or was going to ask us to sponsor an event

/fundraiser. The hidden rule for me was that I would not take the appointment unless I knew that I wanted to work with this person in the first place. No need to "lead" people on without purpose. But they had to pass one final test. That test was how they treat our server for lunch. Most people did not know that the guy in front of them in a polished suit and tie, used to work serving the public at In N Out Burger. If my guest was not polite, professional, and willing to offer respect, then I would never do business with them. It was a black and white rule for me. The service industry has some of the hardest working people on the planet, if you're not willing to give them respect, why should I do the same by giving you, my business. Your actions speak louder than your words when interacting with people.

As business owners, entrepreneurs, professionals, and parents, we must understand that if we want to lead, we must lead by actions, not by mere words. It is through actions that a leader is born and it is through these actions that we can set terrific examples for many others who may choose to work for us or to learn from us.

Fate had to bring this story full circle, and it did. Once, I was at Target, and I was with my eldest daughter, who was still 5 years old. We parked at the very back of the parking lot, not because we couldn't find any spots but because we liked the extra exercise, we would get walking all the way to the front door. At the end of the parking lot, there is no space to put your shopping cart. I always told my daughters that only lazy people don't pick up their trash or put their carts back in the proper location. This day I was distracted by my phone or something grabbing my attention other than the fact that I had just put the shopping cart wheels up in the closest planter. You know what I'm talking about. That's when, and almost immediately, my daughter said:

"Daddy! Are you being lazy? You didn't put the shopping cart back. You told me that only lazy people don't put them back." "You know what? You're right. I did take the easy way, and I felt lazy. I'll be right back."

Since then, I have never ever not put the shopping cart back. This goes all the way back to what Andy said. Do I care about the next person? Yes, I do, and I carry out actions that speak louder than my words. I am thankful that my daughter has also learned enough to hold me accountable for my actions, regardless of how small.

Look at your life and evaluate where your words don't match your actions. Make a change and don't look back. Be a person of action. The rewards are much greater when you're in the game instead of the stands watching and yelling to the players.

Chapter 14

Make It Clear

If you go to get something specific in life, you will end up receiving just that. If you are clouded up, unable to set the right and specific goals, you are probably not going to achieve anything remotely interesting in life.

Earlier in the book, I mentioned SMART goals, being Specific, Measurable, Attainable, Relevant, and Time-bound. If your goals follow that pattern, you have nothing to worry about. However, just because you have goals doesn't mean you will achieve them. The action part comes into play as well, but it is gaining clarity that takes precedence here because if you are not clear on what you want to achieve, you will never know what kind of actions to take. If you do not know what you want to achieve in life, you will never know if you have already achieved them.

I had my health and fitness goals. Then, I had my business goals, investment goals, and eventually my goals to work from home. I was crystal clear about what I wanted in life, and because of that, I knew what I had to do in order to achieve those goals. If you are not clear about them, you are not going to achieve them.

Clarity Equals Achievement

I cannot say it any clearer and simpler than that. People who want to achieve greater things in life do so if they have clarity. I am not only talking about having clarity in business matters either because it applies the same in other areas of life. Whether you are trying to build a relationship, start a business, buy a house, or do any of that, you need clarity, a certainty that allows you to know what exactly you want to achieve. If you are in a relationship, and you do not have a clear idea of where your relationship is heading, it is destined to fail sooner or later. Similarly, if you want to buy a house, and that's your goal, you can buy literally any house on the market, but by bringing in more clarity, such as knowing your budget, what kind of a property you want, how many bedrooms it should have, and every small detail, and almost immediately, your options are now limited, and that's actually good. Now, whatever options you have, are more tailored to your requirements, your vision, and your targets. It makes the entire process a lot easier and eventually sees you buying something that is of genuine value to you and your family.

When you are being grateful for the things that you have, or if you are speaking to yourself about what you want, and you have clarity, you will achieve what you set your mind to.

Having clarity also allows you to become certain. When you have certainty, people see that and can tell immediately if you are someone that they would want to do business with, to interact with, or to get to know. A person who is certain of what they want in life tends to attract a lot more attention than a person who has no idea of what they are supposed to chase in life.

The Yes, The No, The Maybe

In life, you always have a choice to either say yes to something or say no. Despite what many believe, there is no middle ground there. There is no room for “Maybe” because all that will do for you is to keep you second-guessing, observing, and waiting for some magical moment of clarity to arrive. By the time it does, which is rare, you are already too late to cash in on an opportunity.

Think about it this way. You are trying to find yourself a working partner for your firm. There are many potential candidates that turnup, and you go through all the profiles. You would either say yes or no. There won't be any that you would keep as a maybe because that shows a lack of something that you may not be too sure about. If we have learned anything, it is to become certain, and if you find something that doesn't add up or something that feels missing, walk away.

In a similar way, if you were invited to become a partner at a successful firm, you may be excited and end up saying yes to a role that may not be best suited for you. To ensure that things work out fine for you and the firm that you will become a partner of you must ensure that there is clarity. Talk to the decision-maker and get all the information you need, such as what you are expected to do, what your perks and benefits would be, and so on. If something comes up that doesn't work for you, state it clearly that it doesn't. You, as a business owner, professional, or entrepreneur, must draw a line in the sand so that everyone knows what you can do and what you can't do. If you were to give in to the idea "Maybe it wouldn't be that bad," you are likely to find yourself surrounded by worries, stress, and anxiety later on.

The "maybe" stance is what burns through your resources without providing you with any results at the end of the day. It is clarity that ensures you drive the kind of results you need. We like to convince ourselves that we can do something, but at the same time, we try and come up with excuses such as "I don't have the time to do that right now," or "I may need a bit more time to get started." That's the mindset that focuses more on the "but" and the "maybe" instead of coming up with a clear decision.

The Answer is Yes

That's actually the name of my podcast, and now you know why I named it that. To me, having clarity in life is what allows me to do many things, achieve accomplishments that many others can only dream of, and involve myself in a lifestyle that I truly enjoy every single day. It is through this clarity that I can focus my energy on where it matters, and it is also what helps me drive results for my clients.

Whenever I enter a spartan race, which is challenging at times, I know that people walk into the race thinking to themselves "Maybe, I might be able to finish the race," or "Maybe, I just might end up somewhere near the top." When I enter, I know I will finish the race, and I know I will be at the top, not near it, not close to it, but right there on the podium.

We live in a society that is filled with successful people, especially in sports. This is because we have the technology now that we never had before. However, it could have gone the other way had people, in the past, said no to incorporating these technologies into sports, and the same would have been the case if they were confused on whether or not they should use these technologies. They said yes, and here we are, a few decades later, winning records and gold medals every time our people go out to compete in the world of sports.

The Yes People

I had the pleasure to be around a lot of those professional athletes and race car drivers. They all had the "yes" mentality, and they would never doubt their capabilities. They would always enter an event knowing that they would give their best and achieve the results they want. I have never met a single successful athlete that thought "Maybe, I'll win this time."

These are the kind of people you want to surround yourself with when it comes to business. You need the people who say yes as opposed to maybe. You need the people who do not make any excuses at the start line because if they do so, they will never be able to take you across the finish line.

Who you surround yourself with is who you are going to become!

One of my first sales meetings that I had attended at Ketel One vodka, there was a salesman named Ernie Brodbeck giving a presentation. He was in his late 60s, been in the business the last 40 plus years, and he dressed to impress. The guy was a legend at sales.

As the meeting went on, he stood up, took off his polished and expensive shoes, and showed everyone what was underneath the shoes. The soles were worn off completely. He pointed to them and said:

"You're never going to make any sales unless you are willing to go out and hit the streets and wear out the soles of these shoes."

Soon, I left that company and started my own. That message by Ernie stuck with me my entire career. I realized that as an entrepreneur, I needed to be outselling, to be relevant. What I found in being out there, doing the hard work, is that 9 out of 10 times, it led to sales. If I bumped into someone I already knew, it would lead to opportunities.

If you are not out, doing the hard work, making your presence felt in the business, you will not succeed. Too often, people just want to sit behind their fancy desks and a laptop and pretend like they are being successful and achieving whatever it is that they are hoping for. However, if you remove the hard work, there is no reward, no success, and certainly no achievement.

Hard work is infectious – It spreads fast!

When I ran one of the successful In N Out Burger locations, our hours of operations were 10:30 to 1 AM, with Fridays and Saturdays closing at 1:30 AM. We were pretty firm on that. If anyone closed early, that would cost them their job. As the store garnered success, I realized that at 10 AM, we were all there, ready to start the day early with a half an hour to spare.

"Why don't we open up now? Why wait till the clock hits 10:30?"

We started opening up at 10:20 AM, then 10:15 AM, and, ultimately, we settled for opening up 30 minutes prior to the official opening times. This happened because I motivated my team through bonuses and rewards for their commitment and efforts. At the mere suggestion of opening up early, they rallied up. Why? Because as a leader, I was willing to put in the hard work, and they followed. I was involved in the process of opening the doors up earlier. This is one of the reasons why I was able to have one of the most successful stores in the history of the company.

From all the lessons that we have learned, if we were to apply them to our personal and business lives, we would create a culture for others to follow. If you are going to take these lessons and apply them to become an entrepreneur, the culture you will create will be that of success. You will cut out the draggers. You will promote working harder, hitting the streets, getting the job done, having the yes attitude, having the right actions that speak louder than words, and above all, have clarity on what you want yourself and your business to be. It could also be a culture within your department if you are working for someone else or a culture that will represent you and your family in society.

Hard work comes when it is typically least expected. When you are in the restaurant business, you would know the ins and outs of the business and carry on with your daily routine activities. However, hard work comes when the unexpected arrives at your doorstep. Often, it comes during an interaction with a customer, with one of the vendors, and the same is the case in personal life where you may see something unexpected in the neighborhood or at home. Doing the right thing is always the right thing, and often, that comes as a sacrifice (in the form of hard work). Recognizing that you are in that process, and knowing what you need to do at that moment can actually turn out to be one of the most critical moments in your life.

Don't look at the situation as yet more hard work, but treat it as an opportunity to obtain better results. Once you set your mind to it and approach it with that positive attitude, you will come out the other end thinking "You know what? It wasn't as hard as I thought."

Chapter 15

Look Up and Make Friends in Line

Years ago, I had a business partner. He was one of those guys who would talk everybody. He would engage in conversations with strangers longer than any of us would have time for. I have always considered myself as a nice guy, one who respected and cared for others, and I never really disliked anybody. But I was not that "guy" that would strike up a random conversation with strangers.

At some point in our relationship, Sean gave me that look that he needed to help me understand another "core" value in life. He said "Jim you never know who you will meet in public and what that may lead to. You can travel the world and learn more about the place you are in by just striking up a conversation with a stranger". I saw his point but I'm not sure I was ready to become the mayor of every town we traveled to.

What I did understand is how important it could be to reach out and meet the people that surround me. Whether that's in line at the coffee shop, or buying groceries at the local market. Its time to look up and get off our phone screens.

To be honest, it is getting more difficult to do that as time progresses, especially because of social media. Almost every single person these days are glued to their cell phones and tablets. The entire practice of saying hello, has become a lot harder. However, one thing to note is the fact that your single effort to say hello to someone may just be what that other person needs to kick-start their day. This is particularly applicable if you have done your gratitude exercise in the morning and are out to get coffee and feeling positive. Instead of hiding your great mood, turn around and say good morning and hello to the people around you.

That is where you might make a difference. While it may not be evident right away, there will come a time where people will be waiting for you to say hello to them. They will remember the impression you left on them, that sense of positivity that you passed on to them. That is where opportunities will also start presenting themselves for you.

Don't be afraid to look up in line and say hello. Whether or not someone says it back to you, do this and I assure you;

you will start witnessing opportunities of a completely different kind. You may find new friends, connect with potential customers and clients, and may even open doors to newer opportunities.

If I am at a checkout stand, getting helped by the employees at the retail store, I have made it a habit to ask them how their day is going. It doesn't take much, but you'd be surprised to find out that most people are pretty happy with their jobs, and some may actually appreciate your efforts and tell you how nobody has asked them in a very long time.

It goes back to giving back to the community. What you are effectively doing is giving some of that positivity back to the people working. That positivity that you give out will come back to you or the next customer, and it will continue to flow. Think about it. Just asking how their day is going can actually serve as a pivot point for them, allowing them to step out of their negativity and into positivity.

We, as human beings, have distanced ourselves from such practices significantly. There was a time where we would greet every person that walked across the street. Now, if we wave to someone, they'd be surprised and somewhat shocked, wondering why on earth are we waving to them.

When I leave this small country town and work in the bigger cities, it becomes clear to me how unfriendly we can be, and have become. It is a great opportunity to remind people that we are all the same. We all must take some time out from the day to wave at people, greet them, and ask how their day is going. It isn't much, but it is certainly going to create a culture.

People underestimate the power of relationships and the power of connecting the dots. A person might say hello to someone in a line, and might even ask them what they do for a living. Let's imagine that this person sells computer parts for a living. You may not need any computer parts for yourself, but you might recall someone who does. All you have to do now is to connect the dots and help someone have their computer fixed while helping the other generating more business. Just because of a single hello, you were able to pass along that strategic contact.

Chapter 16

Health and Fitness Goals

"Master Mortality"

Jack Donovan

We have an obligation to be the best human beings that we can possibly be, and a very critical part of that is our health and fitness. The healthier and fitter we are, the better our business will be. In simpler words, if I do not have the energy levels to work the 8 hours shift, I am not going to do a good job.

To me, I feel like it is my personal obligation to be the healthiest and fittest I can be, as a father, as an entrepreneur, as a coach, and as a human being for the people that rely on me to get the job done. The more regimented my physical fitness routine is, the better I am at business. I love the #75Hard program because it requires 5 mandates per day. I have to read 10 pages of non-fiction every day. I have to drink a gallon of water, do 2 workouts for 45 minutes (One mandatory outside), take a self-portrait of myself, and avoid sugar or any kind of alcohol. On top of that, I must have some kind of food regiment. If you miss one item from the list, you have to start over.

I found myself at my best, mentally, physically, when I am on #75Hard. This program puts in play a series of mandates in your life that will eventually bring results that would astonish you and help you achieve goals a lot quicker. Not to mention the program is free!

People look at the spartan races and believe it is something that they cannot achieve. It is arguably the toughest test of physical fitness and mental toughness out there. This physical race, brimming with obstacles, is designed to help us not only feel more fit but also to overcome our fears and scenarios that may otherwise unnerve and unsettle us. It gives us something to look back upon to build strength in our minds later in life. It can be accomplished with the right effort.

When I look at my ability to run for 24 hours, in sub-zero temperatures in Iceland, I know that I can do anything in business and in my personal life. If I can maintain health and fitness to do that race, I can easily maintain my energy levels to go through 8 hours of work, at my optimum performance levels. Through physical fitness and through business, I am the best version of myself, and that is why I am not afraid to go out there and do the hard work myself.

We achieve success often by how we feel, and if our best version of ourselves is healthy, we are bound to be successful. If you wake up in the morning and see yourself in the mirror and you like what you see, you are going to have a great day. However, the converse is also true.

If I can get up every morning and spend 20 minutes on my fitness, that time is going to be carried into my business life as well. Not only will I see my body transitioning for the better, but my business will become better too. If I lack the energy to go down to the gym, I am going to approach my business the same way.

I love talking about progress because people usually put things off. They feel like they are far too preoccupied to spare enough time for other important aspects of life. This is something that can happen with entrepreneurs in the business as well. While you may have planned to establish a business, you still don't because you are trying to make enough money from your current business. This means that you must only focus on your current business and almost forget completely about newer goals. Once again, I advise people to use the 5-

minute a day formula to help them get moving in the right direction.

By sharing my progress, by letting the world know what I have achieved, I end up motivating others to step out of their comfort zones and start doing something productive and meaningful as well. It always takes one person to take the lead to allow millions of people to follow.

If you dedicate just 5 minutes of your time to your business, and do that every day, I assure you that by the time you hit the end of the 2 months mark, you will have made up plenty of ground. You will no longer be a beginner or someone who is still caught up in the “Maybe” phase. You would have actually taken action that would compound into something tangible. That’s real progress.

Look over and above the fear of starting and just START.

If you do something for two weeks, it becomes a habit. Andy Frisella is the mind behind the #75Hard program. The idea is to follow the same regiment for 75 days and find yourself completely transformed into this positive, healthy, and energetic person. To be honest, you get a lot more in value. Not only do you get to set new and healthier habits, but you move forward in life to crush those goals and look for more challenging ones. Instead of just two weeks, he goes the extra mile and does this for 75 days.

Whether you are trying to regain your fitness, or you are trying to bring a change in life and in business, the #75Hard program is one incredible way to move forward. It allows you to become the best version of yourself and building some real mental toughness.

The importance of what you will learn through this program is the importance of integrity to yourself. While you can finish the program easily because you are literally not accountable to anyone else except yourself. This means that you can easily cut some corners, cheat a little, and still claim you went through the day with the regime, and no one would know. However, if you are not putting in 100% of your commitment towards yourself and your business, you will end up with the same results; nobody will know who you are, and that's bad news for any business owner. To make an impact, you need to honor your commitments, put in the work, go through the regiment and make it a habit. The same will spill over into your business because now, you will ensure every commitment is met till its very end. You will no longer be cutting corners or taking the easier way out, and that will eventually get you the attention you need. Why? Because now, you are a person of integrity and commitment.

Conclusion

I am intentionally writing this final chapter looking out on the Las Vegas strip from a room on the 56th floor of the Trump Hotel. Several circumstances put me here today but all I can think about is getting back home to my girls. There was a time in my life where this would have been a moment worth living and talking about. Don't get me wrong, it's a great hotel and the view is one of the best in Vegas. However, nothing that I am doing at this very moment aligns with my values except my internal drive to get home ASAP. Instead, this will serve as a final reminder of who I was and who I don't want to ever be again. So again, I have intentionally put myself in this position to wrap up my book. Lesson learned, dummy tax paid, so you don't have to.

Being an entrepreneur, or business owner, is pretty much anyone with ambitions dream. Only a handful of those who have the heart and soul to put in the efforts, the dedication, the sweat, and blood, actually become successful.

Life is a one-time thing, and there is no such thing as a do-over. Once we are done, we are done. When you think about it that way, it does make you wonder. It does connect with something deep within you, forcing you to ask yourself whether you are doing enough or have done enough in life. In most cases, the answer is no.

Our lives aren't just about being born, growing up, and then to pay taxes and bills for the rest of our lives. That's neither our purpose nor the only goal. Our lives are meant to be far more significant than that. We are empowered by God with gifts, abilities, and with talents that hide within us. It takes time, practice, and some good digging to figure out who we really are, what do we do best, and how we can use that to our advantage.

You can be an athlete who might have decided to have a change of career. No problem there. You may already be a business owner, but might have decided to switch industries, and that may not be a big deal either. In fact, you might as well be an employee, working those usual 9 to 5 hours, traveling through the big cities, hoping to land a decent job, and you might have decided one night "I need a change in life." Well, the good news is that everything is possible, if you are willing enough to invite the change, to be the change.

The first thing to understand is that we are who we are, and whatever that image may look like, it will be reflected in the business we do. Each one of us is unique, and that is primarily why I always find the values that my clients have. It is through having clarity and core values that someone can move forward in life because almost every decision we make for ourselves, and for our families, revolve around those values. If you haven't figured them out yet, get started right away.

Throughout this book, I have provided multiple stories, personal experiences, and more, and all of that can be boiled down to one simple thing; to "Live Life Driven", you need to first start the engine that drives your life, and that starts with faith.

You may be a Christian, a Muslim, a Jew, and it literally doesn't matter. What you need is to have faith in something, call it a higher power, God, or the Universe. There is something out there that is constantly providing for you in ways you cannot imagine. However, to receive that, you need to start having faith that everything will work out for you. You need to believe because what you believe is what you will achieve.

If you do good in life by putting the kinder sentiments out there in the universe, you are destined to receive more kindness in return. Of course, not everything will be based on finances, but the principle remains the same.

Before starting your big venture, know what your strengths are and what your weaknesses are. Everyone has them, and there is no reason to shy away from them. The sooner you figure them out, the quicker you can move towards progress.

Whether you are doing good already, or have just started, be grateful. We are living through a time where the world was plagued with sheer negativity and is still struggling to come out of that darkness. It is up to us to spread that light, spread the positivity, and invite positive results in our lives.

When you do start, stop worrying about what your competitors are doing. Put on your blinders and race towards the finish line just like the horses do when they are brought out to race. There is no point in trying to sneak into what your competitor is doing or what kind of technology they are using. If you know your craft, and you are a master at it, that's all you need to proceed.

For your goals, write them down. Be clear, and write them down following the SMART rule:

- Be specific
- Be measurable
- Be attainable
- Be relevant
- Be time-bound

Say these goals out loud to yourself and for the universe to hear because, believe it or not, the universe does hear you. Whatever you put out there, it will be heard, and it will be manifested for you in your life. Therefore, stop with the negative self-talk and start using positivity instead.

We all make mistakes, and that's part of being a human being. If you make a decision, stick to it and ride it all the way through. Whether it is the right one or the wrong one, that's for us to learn later. If you find yourself in a tough spot, or you need some guidance, be sure to seek help. In fact, get in touch with me, and I would be more than happy to assist you as your coach.

The people you see at the very top are the people that hold a treasure of opportunities for people like you and me. Instead of being intimidated by them, approach them, get to know them, and seek opportunities that will benefit both parties mutually. Do not shy away from hard work because, contrary to popular belief, working smart will only get you far enough but it is hard work that will help you go all the way.

Finally, don't speak; act! Your actions are what dictate how others perceive you as a person. If you do something good, they will know you to be a good person. However, if you do something bad and still claim you did that for good intentions, you will still be viewed as a negative character. For an entrepreneur and a business owner, it is imperative that you take actions that speak for you.

With that said, it is now time for me to part ways. I do hope that this book has helped you gain some valuable insights into my life and has also provided you with a rich source of information and knowledge. There is no point in having knowledge and keeping it to yourself. If this book has helped anyone change their lives for the better, even one, I know I'd have served my purpose.

Remember, only you can give yourself ***the freedom to say yes*** to a new life. If you can master that, then you are ready to drive your life wherever you want to go.

Thank You

My life has been influenced by many people, family, friends, leaders, and entrepreneurs although a few come to mind every time.

My Grandfather, Jack Linscott, taught me at 13 years old that if you have time to lean, there is time to clean. He also taught me the value of a dollar and how it feels to get paid “cash”. He will always be in my memory

My Brother Mark Taylor has been my biggest life influence for a variety of reasons. He taught me how to say “No” when it's important. He showed me how to be a husband, a father, and he is one of the most caring people I have ever known. Thank you, Mark.

Coming from a two-family childhood (Two Moms), I learned to love and care deeply from Diane, and I learned how to bust “balls” and not get pushed around by Sherry. My other brother Scott and Sister Tanya have taught me loyalty and the value of family no matter where you are on the planet.

Thanks to my dad, Dearyl Riley, for instilling work ethic and doing any job that came my way. His tools will live in my garage forever and continue to have a purpose in my life. Pun intended.

The most important person I could Thank in this life was a gift from God because I cannot see it any other way.

Samantha said "Yes" to me more than eight years ago and is the mother of our two incredible daughters Dearylin and Reagan. Samantha showed me her love through her actions and how she cared for others without thinking. The most touching moment was the night she met my dad for the first time. He was in his last days of fighting Cancer. Samantha treated him like the father she would have had if he never passed. Her thoughts, questions, and conversation solidified my love for her and who she is as a person. I am blessed to have Samantha in my life…

Other people that matter: David Meltzer, John Fuller, Rick Johnson, Andy Bardon, Traci Taylor, Peter Jacobsen, Bob Grammen, Bill Eldien, John Rice, Alan Rago, Phil Limon, Leslie Zann, Andy Frisella, Ed Mylett, Sean Whalen, Rachel Svoboda, Robert Hymers, Sonny and Heather Tudor, Jeff Michalak, Cameron Steele, Rico Austin, Kyle Turley, Tavi, Jim Beaver, Sal Fish, Jordan Nicols, Dana Zamalloa, John Rice, Gary Mills, Cory Ellenson, Arete Syndicate, Olen Hamilton, Paul Garrett, Jeff Foster, Ryan Arciero, Pistol Pete, Sergio Zuniga, Bill Walton, and many more. Froggy – the next chapter is yours!

Special Thanks to Rod Kuntz and Samantha Riley for editing the final drafts of this book. You are both amazing.

LIVELIFEDRIVEN

Jim Riley has spent his entire life saying yes to career changes and unique opportunities that align with his foundational values.

Riley runs a successful, consulting business in Kalispell, Montana. Known for supplying value to clients by providing strategic recommendations, Jim Riley is known for smart strategic thinking, insightful operations, successful business growth and high pressure transitions.

Jim is currently the host of two successful podcasts. "The Answer is "Yes" podcast features business leaders discussing both the power of saying "yes" and the decisions that made them successful. "The Liberty of Lose" podcast features local and national public figures discussing current politics and where the country is heading.

In addition, Riley actively consults for several successful companies and is known for helping businesses through transitional phases, marketing strategy, sales improvements, public relations, providing innovation and facilitating operational improvements.
Riley oversees two of his own business and has an extensive background in marketing, food and beverage, and everything in between.

Well known work includes time spent with In-N-Out, Ketel One Vodka, Galardi Group, Booth Creek Ski Holdings, Azunia Tequila, and Baja United Group.

Jim Riley is a leading advocate for conservative political actions as School Board Trustee in Smith Valley District 89. He is a popular speaker on the subjects of education, veterans, 2nd Amendment Rights, freedom of religion, small government, public land use, legal immigration, the constitution, pro-life, first responders, and the Save the Cowboy movement in Montana.

JIM RILEY

CONSULTANT | SPEAKER | BUSINESS COACH

School Board Trustee, Smith Valley District 89, Kalispell, Montana

---

Jim@LiveLifeDriven.com | 406-257-1637 | www.livelifedriven.com

Made in the USA
Monee, IL
25 March 2025

14607641R10095